Family Walks
in
East Cheshire

Published by Sigma Leisure – an imprint of
Sigma Press, Stobart House, Pontyclerc, Penybanc Road, Ammanford, Carmarthenshire SA18 3HP.

British Library Cataloguing in Publication Data
A CIP record for this book is available from the British Library.

ISBN: 978-1-85058-903-7

Typesetting and Design by: Sigma Press, Ammanford, Carms

Cover photograph: Astbury in springtime © Jean Warham

Photographs: © Jean Warham

Illustrations: © Karen Ross

Maps: Reproduced by permission of Ordnance Survey on behalf of HMSO ©Crown Copyright 2005. Ordnance Survey licence number 100032058

Printed by: TJ International Ltd, Padstow, Cornwall

Disclaimer: the information in this book is given in good faith and is believed to be correct at the time of publication. No responsibility is accepted by either the author or publisher for errors or omissions, or for any loss or injury howsoever caused. Only you can judge your own fitness, competence and experience. Do not rely solely on sketch maps for navigation: we strongly recommend the use of appropriate Ordnance Survey (or equivalent) maps.

Family Walks
in
East Cheshire

Jean Warham

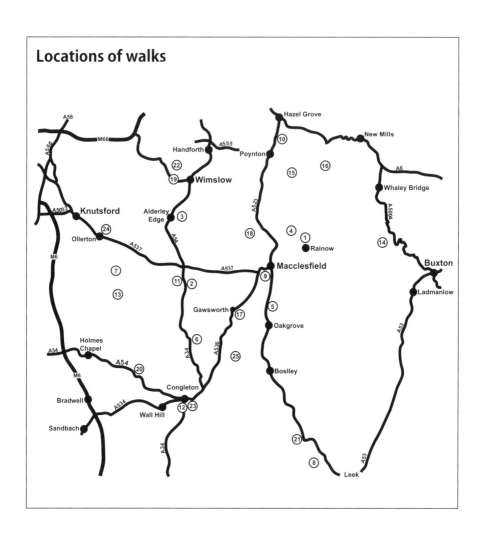

Contents

Dedication
This book is dedicated to Roy, without whose love and support this book would not have been written.

Acknowledgements
Acknowledgement and appreciation go to all those friends who have shared these walks with me over the years. I take this opportunity to say how much I have enjoyed their company, and thank them for their encouragement to record these walks for all to enjoy for years to come.

Introduction

The walks are all circular, and about 3 to 4 miles long. They are never too steep or difficult, and can be walked at an easy pace in about one and a half to two hours, allowing time to admire the view or look at the birds or wild flowers along the way. They are all chosen for their variety of scenery, including particular places of beauty or interest. Some of the walks are of particular interest in certain seasons. This book tells you when these walks are at their best.

Footpaths – All the walks in this book follow recognised footpaths. They will be marked with signposts and footpath markers.

Yellow footpath arrow markers – When crossing the countryside, watch for the yellow arrow markers, which will show you the direction the footpath will take.

Maps – The maps are drawn to scale but do not include all the details. They are there to give an overall view of directions and relative lengths of sections. The fine detail is in the text.

Stiles – A lot of the old stiles are being replaced with small 'kissing' gates, so where the text says 'stile' it could be either a stile or a small gate. Some of the walks have no stiles on them, only gates.

Parking – You can usually park in pub car parks if you intend having your lunch there. They are generally happy for you to park in their car park while you have your walk.

Safe walking on roads

Most of the walks are on footpaths. When they do go onto a road, they mostly use very quiet roads, but sometimes part of a walk will go along a road which has some traffic. To take care on these country roads, walk on the right of the road, so that you can see traffic that is approaching on your side of the road, then if necessary, you can step onto the grass verge. EXCEPTING: that if the road curves to the right, walk on the left of the road until the road straightens out again. This gives you a much better view of oncoming traffic. Also drivers will see you sooner.

Country Code

- Do not stray from official footpaths, which are marked
- Do no damage to crops or livestock
- Avoid damaging gates, fences, walls and hedges
- Leave all gates closed if you found them closed, or open if you found them open
- Keep dogs under control
- Take only photographs, leave only footprints

1. The Apprentice Path Walk

This is one of the shorter walks. It is less than three miles long, but it is a lovely walk, not to be missed. It goes from Rainow to Bollington and has some of the most beautiful views around Macclesfield.

For part of the walk you can see the Bollington folly 'White Nancy'. This has always been a landmark for Bollington. It is normally painted white, but in the past, it has on various occasions been painted by local people who remained anonymous, then was later restored to its official white colour.

Distance	2½ miles
Allow	1¼ hours
Terrain	Dry underfoot , even after rain
By car	From Macclesfield, drive up Hurdsfield Road, the B5470. At Rainow turn left at the Robin Hood pub, go past the entrance to the pub car park, and then turn right and park in the road behind the pub.
Map	Philip's Ordnance Survey Street Atlas Cheshire Page 88 C3

The walk

Start by walking in the same direction as you were driving. At the grassy triangle turn left onto the bridle path. This is called Oakenbank Lane, because it used to be an old packhorse route from Rainow to Bollington. As you walk uphill on this path you will find that it has the loveliest views, and you will see White Nancy on your left.

After just over a mile you come to houses on your right and two footpaths on the left, together. The first is marked as the Gritstone Trail. The second one just has a footpath sign. Take the first one. Climb through the gap in the wall and down the steps which are set into the other side of the wall. Go down some steps to a pretty little stream on your left, and then up the steps in the path. Go through the small gate with the farmhouse of

Apprentice Path Walk

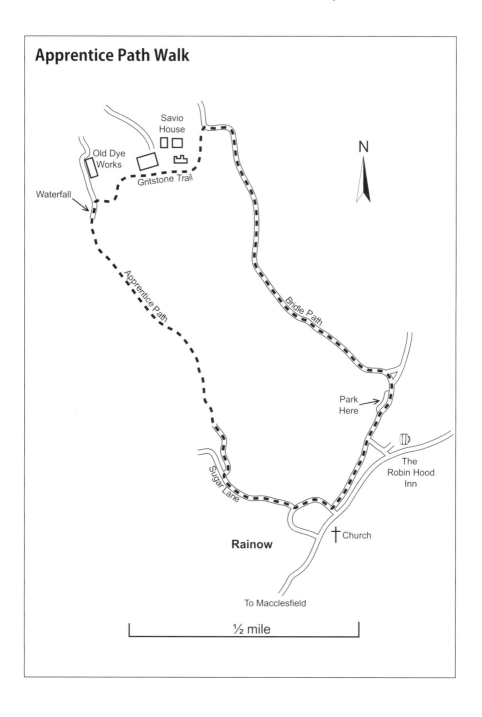

Higher Ingersley Farm on your left. Continue along this path and you will pass the back gate to Savio House on your right, with a complex of buildings. (The main entrance is on the other side.) You will then come to a stone wall with a stile of the type where stone steps are set into the wall. Cross this and you will see another on your right, which leads to a cottage. Go past this and go straight ahead and through a small wooden gate, and then bear right to follow the path, which leads down into the valley. Take time to admire the views which are very good here. The path goes through two small metal gates and then down some steps. The path continues downhill and then over a bridge which crosses the river Dean, before reaching the final small metal gate. This leads you onto a narrow, quiet road. If you look to the right you will see where the old Bollington dye works stood, with the river running underneath it, because water was needed for the process. The road to the right leads into Bollington.

Turn left and follow the road. At the end of this road is Waulkmill Farm. On the right there is a beautiful waterfall – a hidden gem. Continue on past the waterfall and you will enter a field.

This is the start of the apprentice path. The entire path had been paved for the apprentices to walk from the works and mills at Bollington to the church at Rainow every Sunday. Much of this paving is still in place. The path crosses several fields. There are stiles between the fields, which are of the old type. They consist of slabs of stone, which you have to squeeze between. The apprentice path follows the line of the ridge of Kerridge, which is on your right. The views are spectacular.

The waterfall at Waulkmill Farm

The path eventually comes out behind a row of cottages, onto Sugar lane, where you turn left. At the top of Sugar lane turn left onto the road called 'Round Meadow'. Pass the first turning on the left then turn left at the next one, which is Stocks Lane. There is a reconstructed set of stocks here. Go straight on to where you parked your car.

Refreshments

To turn your car round on this narrow road, the easiest way is to drive up to the grassy triangle where you can easily turn round. You can have lunch in the Robin Hood pub, or go past the entrance to the pub car park and then turn left onto the main road. After one mile turn left into Blaze hill, which is the first turning on the left. This will take you down into Bollington. The first part of this road has views which are not to be missed. When you come to the roundabout in Bollington you can turn left into Church Street and go to the Church House, or go straight on through Bollington to reach the Cock and Pheasant at the far end of Bollington. Both are recommended.

Robin Hood Inn The, Church Lane, Rainow, Macclesfield SK10 5XE
Church House Inn, 24 Church Street, Bollington SK10 5PY
Cock and Pheasant, 15 Bollington Road, Bollington, Macclesfield SK10 5EJ

2. Redesmere to Siddington Church

This is a lovely walk through the countryside; with open views, and wooded paths. At the start you can enjoy the beauty of the lake with its great variety of water fowl. There is an information board to help you to identify the various species.

Distance	4½ miles
Allow	2¼ hours
Terrain	This walk is suitable in all seasons.
By car	In Macclesfield, take the road to Broken Cross (A537). At the roundabout, turn left into Gawsworth Road, then after a few yards turn right into Pexhill Road (B5392). After three and a half miles you come to the A34. Turn right then take the first turning on your right, which is Redesmere Lane. Park next to the lake.
Map	Philip's Ordnance Survey Street Atlas Cheshire Page 110 A2

The walk

When you leave the car, walk up Redesmere Lane with the lake on your left. About 100 yards up the road you come to a stile on your left. Cross this and walk straight on over a small field, then cross over another stile. Continue along a fenced path until it comes to a junction with one path going straight on and the other one turning right. Turn right here. This fenced path leads you on to a driveway. There are large wrought iron gates to the left. Turn right, and walk down the driveway, which then joins a narrow road, called Fanshawe Lane. Continue straight on. Pass some thatched cottages and other houses on your left. There is a stream running alongside the road on your right. It is called Fanshawe Brook.

When you come to the T-junction with Redesmere Lane, go across the road, over a stile, then up a short slope. This slope is usually a little wet, but easy to cross. At the top of the slope turn left. Cross a stile into a second field and go straight on. Cross another stile into the third field.

Redesmere to Siddington Church

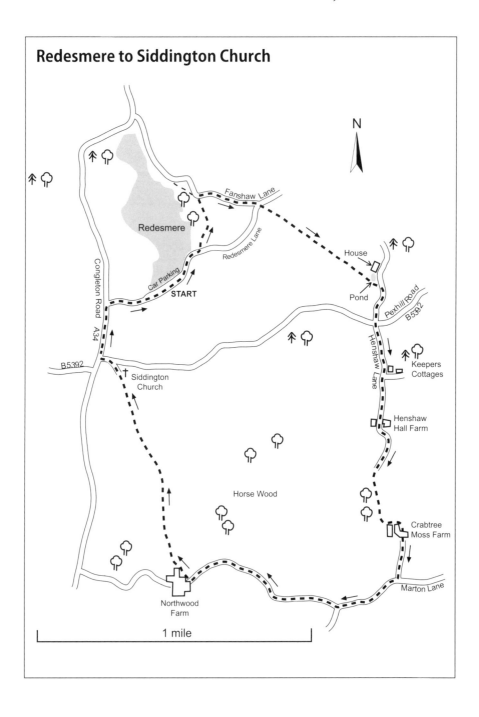

You will see only trees ahead. Bear right. Halfway down the fence on the right, go through the gap, cross a concrete pathway and head straight on to a stile. Cross this stile which brings you into a large field. Go straight across this field. The next stile takes you into a very small field with a house straight ahead. Turn to the right. Pass the house, and then a pond on your left, then cross a stile, turn left and cross another stile. This brings you onto the road which leads to houses. Turn right onto the road. Go straight onwards to a cross roads with Pexhill Road.

Go straight across Pexhill Road and then straight on, down Henshaw Lane. When the road forks, the left fork goes to Keepers Cottages and Coach House, take the right fork, which is labelled as going to Henshaw Hall Farm. Pass a large house on your left called Henshaw House, then a much older house which is the farmhouse of Henshaw Hall farm. The other farm buildings are on your right. The path you are following will then curve round to the left. Look at the splendid view to your left before the path dips down and passes through Moss Wood.

Moss Wood

Continue straight on for about half a mile on this wide path through some woods then some very pleasant countryside until you reach Crabtree Moss Farm. When you reach Crabtree Moss Farm, the path will take an S shape, turning first left, then right, and then into the grounds of, and onto the driveway, of a large house. Walk down the drive, passing the house on your right. Continue down the drive to the road. This is Marton Lane, which becomes School Lane further down. Turn right into the road.

After a short walk along the road, just before reaching the buildings of Marton Gate Farm on your left, turn right into a wide entrance to a farm gate, set back a little from the road. After passing through the gate, continue straight on. Keep following the farm track. After the first part, most of the track is surfaced with concrete. After about half a mile it reaches Northwood Farm.

The path then turns right just before the farm buildings. Continue to follow this path until the concrete runs out and then go straight on to the fence on the far side and you will see a stile on your left. Cross the stile into a small field, and then turn right to go to the next stile. Cross this stile into another small field, and then follow the path that curves round to your left. Cross another stile to take you into a large grassed field, and

Passing fields of yellow rapeseed flowers

then continue up the slope. Go straight on across another two fields, over another concrete farm track, then across a very small field to another stile. Keep going straight on across another two fields and you will see Siddington Church straight ahead.

Go in through a small gate, cross a very small field, and then walk through the church grounds, past the church which is on your right, then down the church's drive to Pexhill Road. Cross the road and turn left. On your right, in the field, you will see the remains of what used to be the mill pond. Walk the few yards to the end of Pexhill Road, cross the A34, and then turn right. You will pass a building on your left which used to be the old mill, and then pass over the stream which used to turn the mill wheel. Turn right into the first road on your right, which takes you back to your car.

Refreshments

When you drive back to the A34, turn left. Drive to The Davenport Arms on your right at Marton, or drive a little further on to The Waggon and Horses on your left.

Davenport Arms, Congleton Road, Marton, Macclesfield SK11 9HF
Wagon and Horses, Manchester Road (A34), Eaton, Nr. Congleton CW12 2JD

3. Alderley Edge

Alderley Edge is quite high up, so there are stunning views on this walk. In the autumn the colours of the leaves in the Alderley Edge woods are worth seeing. In the spring you can look out for the wildflowers in the hedgerows. You will see the white flowers of the greater stichwort and the red of the red campion, and also bluebells in the hedgerows. Alderley Edge Woods are preserved as a National Trust site, because of its natural beauty.

Distance	3¾ miles
Allow	1 hour 50 minutes
Terrain	This walk can be made shorter by continuing to walk to the end of Bradford Lane. This walk is sheltered from the wind on windy days, and shaded from the sun on hot sunny days. The autumn colours on this walk are well worth seeing.
By car	From Macclesfield, take Prestbury Road (B5087) which goes to Alderley Edge. After you pass Slade Lane on your left, the next road on the left, which forks off, is Finlow Hill Lane. Turn left into Finlow Hill Lane and park in one of the three lay-bys
Map	Philip's Ordnance Survey Street Atlas Cheshire Page 85 F3

The walk

From the lay-by, continue to walk in the direction you were driving until the road turns right. At this point, turn left, and cross a stile. Walk along a path which has a hedge on your right. On your left there is initially a wire fence, then for the whole length of this path there is a splendid panoramic view of the rolling Cheshire countryside, with farms and fields, and the hills of the Peak District forming a backdrop in the distance.

When you reach the road, which is Slade Lane, cross the stile, go down a few steps to the road, then turn right into Slade Lane. Continue to the T-junction at the end of Slade Lane then turn right onto Hocker Lane. This is a very quiet lane, which is more like a wide path. After about fifteen minutes you will come to a T-junction with Bradford Lane. Turn right onto Bradford Lane, which you will find has a cobbled surface. While you walk up Bradford Lane, look out for a wooden signpost on your left, pointing to a stile and a footpath. It is easy to miss. If Bradford Lane runs out of cobbles, you have gone too far.

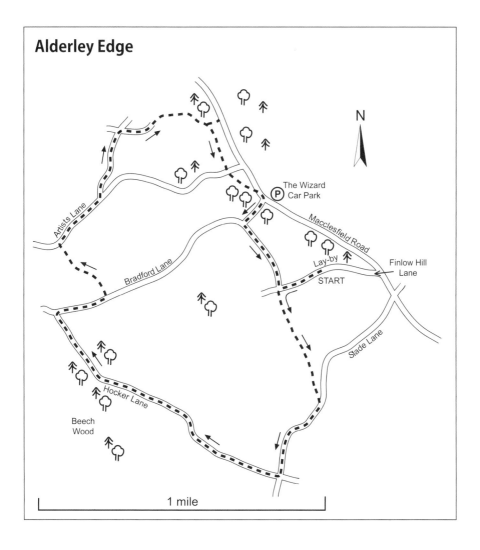

Autumn leaf fall in Alderley Edge

At the signpost, turn left, go a few yards then cross a stile which was hidden from the lane. Continue straight on, following the path, across two small fields, then through a small wood. This brings you out on Artists Lane. Turn right. Artists Lane goes uphill slightly. After you walk round the bend in the road you will see a wide footpath that forks off the road, on the left. Go down this footpath.

Initially this is a wide, tree-lined footpath but it becomes narrower. When you have passed the trees you come to a crossroads of footpaths. The one on the left leads to a gate a few yards away. Take the right turning. This path curves round gently to the left. Go past two narrow footpaths off on your right, and take the wider path. This is marked with a yellow

The carved owl in Artists Lane

arrow. Following this path, it then curves to the right and goes between a stone National Trust sign on your left, and a large fallen tree on your right. There is a notice board next to the fallen tree which tells you about the history of Hagg Cottage. Continue straight on up the slope. After about 100 yards it divides into a bridleway on the right and a footpath on the left. Take the bridleway on the right.

Continue on through Alderley Edge woods, bearing right so that you will come out in Artists Lane. Go straight across the road, and then back into woods on the other side. This will bring you out on the main road which leads to Macclesfield, just before the turning up Bradford Lane. Turn right into Bradford Lane. Follow it until it turns left, with only a narrow lane going straight on. Turn left here. This will bring you to the top of Finlow Hill Lane, where you started.

Refreshments

Head back towards Macclesfield and soon you will come to a fork left which is signposted for Prestbury, and for Hare Hill. Follow this road into Prestbury, and then go through the village of Prestbury until you come to the Admiral Rodney pub on your left on the far side of the village. If you drive past it and take the next left, you will go into the car park behind the pub. The Admiral Rodney is a charming old world pub, with low beams and lots of character.

Alternatively, if you prefer a larger pub, you could go to the Blacksmiths Arms at Henbury. If you drive back towards Macclesfield, you will find it on the main road (A537) which goes from Monks Heath to Broken Cross at Macclesfield. It is a much bigger pub, with a different cuisine.

Ye Olde Admiral Rodney Inn, New Road, Prestbury, Macclesfield SK10 4HP
Blacksmiths Arms, Chelford Road, Henbury, Macclesfield SK11 9PG

4. Kerridge

The flagstones near the start of this walk were paved for the apprentices who used to work in the mills of Bollington. They can be slippery if it has rained recently. There are several of the old 'squash' stiles on this walk, which consist of two stone slabs which you have to squeeze between.

The first half of this walk follows the Ridge of Kerridge on your left. This was called Key Ridge, and it is where Kerridge got its name. Before the Second World War, there was a windmill on this ridge. It had been moved from Windmill Street in Macclesfield. During the war the Germans used the windmill as a landmark to line up for their approach to bomb Manchester. So the Americans dismantled it, and said it would be rebuilt after the war, but it was never rebuilt. They used the stone as hardcore to build the runway of the American air base at Burtonwood, near Liverpool.

Distance	3 miles
Allow	1½ hours
Terrain	Best not to do this walk after recent rain because the flagstones at the start can be slippery when wet.
By car	From Macclesfield take the Silk Road (A523) northwards. When you reach the first turning to Bollington, turn right. After a few yards, turn right again into Clarke Lane. Continue on until Clarke Lane turns left and becomes Oak Lane, which leads into Kerridge. Pass two roads on your right, then you will come to Hollin Hall, set back from the road on your left. The road you are on is now called Jackson Lane. Just before Hollin Hall, on your right, is a small free car park.
Map	Philip's Ordnance Survey Street Atlas Cheshire Page 88 A4

The walk

On leaving the car park turn left, then turn into the first road on your left which is Redway Lane. A short way up here there is a stile on your right.

Kerridge

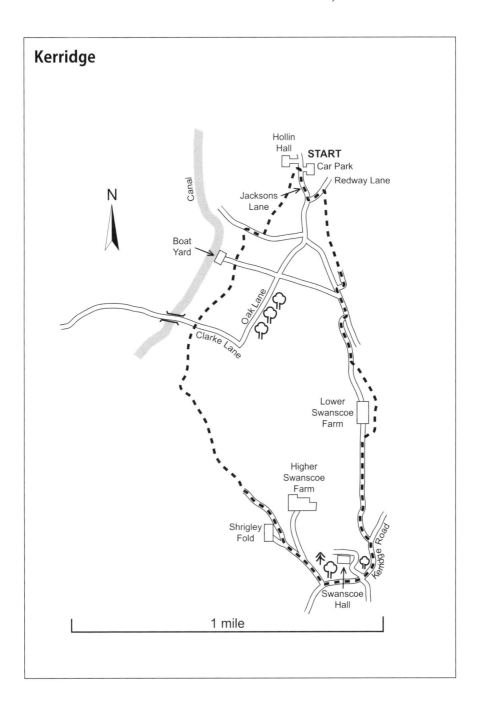

It is a very old and an unusual stile made of large stone blocks. Cross this stile and go straight across the field, walking on a path of flagstones. After passing a stile, there are houses with gardens up a slope on your left, and a view on your right. When the path passes behind houses on your right, it comes to a T-junction where you turn right, and then when you reach the road, which is at the front of the houses, turn left. There is a good view on your right.

Squash stile

Continue straight on, through a gate, and then past a turning on your right. When the path forks, take the right fork, then look out for the carved owl on your left. You then follow a lovely leafy wooded path. There are stunning views on your right.

When you leave the trees behind, go past a footpath on your right, and you will find a gate straight ahead, but the footpath had been diverted from it. Turn left, and then go through the gate on your right, then straight on following the path across the field. You go through another gate which brings you onto a lane. Turn left and follow the lane for a few yards. There is a small gate on your right, then the lane turns right and there are another two small gates on your right. Go through the last one, down about ten steps, and the path will turn left at the bottom. This takes you into a field where you follow the footpath markers diagonally across the field. This brings you out onto the driveway which leads to Lower Swanscoe Farm on your right. All of this diverted path forms a semi-circle to skirt around the farmhouse and outbuildings. Turn left onto the driveway and head away from the farm.

Continue down the drive to the road, and then turn right. Pass some houses. When the road turns left and is labelled as going to Macclesfield, you continue straight on into Swanscoe Lane. Swanscoe Hall is on your right. You will pass another road on the left but keep straight on. When the lane forks, the right fork leads to Higher Swanscoe Farm. Take the left fork. The lane will fork again. The left fork leads to Shrigley Fold Farm.

Take the right fork. After a little while it becomes a path that leads you into a field.

When you reach a very small roofless abandoned house take the stone surfaced path which curves off on your left just before the house. Follow this path until you come to a small pond on your right and a gate and stile ahead, go over the stile and continue straight on following the fence on your left. In the next field pass between two larger ponds, then bear left to a small gate.

When you go through the gate you come into a small narrow lane. Go straight across and through another small gate into a field. The path goes slightly to the right. At the next stile pass between the stone slabs of another 'squash' stile, and then pass a small pond on your right. Continue straight on following the fence on your left until you reach the road. This is Clarke Lane.

Moat Hall Farm, Clarke Lane, Kerridge

Go straight across the road into the field opposite. Follow the fence which is on your right. You come to the driveway which leads to the boatyard on your left. Go straight across this driveway into the field opposite. Head diagonally right to the gate on the other side of this field. This brings you onto a lane. Go straight across the lane into another field. Follow the hedge on your left. This brings you out onto a larger field.

You will see Hollin Hall ahead. On your right there will be a row of houses which are on Jacksons Lane. Veer slightly to the right and then follow the line of large trees which leads you to the corner of the field. You go through a small gate then through a 'squash' stile of two stone slabs, and then out to the road. Cross the road to the car park where your car is parked.

Refreshments

Drive back the way you came, down Oak Lane, then right into Clarke Lane. At the T-junction turn right into Bollington Road. The Cock and Pheasant pub is on your left after about half a mile. You can get an excellent lunch there. Alternatively, at the T-junction turn left. At the roundabout on the Silk Road turn right and then continue straight on to the Legh Arms Carvery at Adlington.

Cock and Pheasant, 15 Bollington Road, Bollington, Macclesfield SK10 5EJ
Legh Arms, London Road, Adlington, Macclesfield SK10 4NA

5. Lyme Green to Sutton

This is a lovely walk because there is a lot of variety in it. The views from the canal to the distant hills are beautiful. The colourful narrow boats on the canal, and the curved stone bridges, make picturesque scenes for the photographer or artist. The reservoir gives an interesting water scene with grebes and other water birds.

Distance	3½ miles
Allow	1¾ hours
Terrain	Chose this walk in dry weather because the section near Sutton Hall can be muddy if there has been a lot of rain recently.
By car	From Macclesfield, take London Road (A523) to the Lyme Green Business Park, and park in the car park, at the far end of the shops.
Map	Philip's Ordnance Survey Street Atlas Cheshire Page 112 B2

The walk

From the car park turn left onto the road and then walk to the end of the road, where there is a footpath on the right hand side, which leads up to Macclesfield canal. When you reach the canal turn left, then walk along the canal towpath with the water on your right. The first bridge you come to, No.45, takes you under London Road. Continue on along the canal to bridge No.44. Go under that bridge and then turn left through the small gate.

Go up the slope and then turn left onto Bullocks Lane. Go across the bridge which goes over the canal. Just the other side of the bridge the first turning on your left is the driveway to Sutton Hall Hotel. Pass this and then a few yards further on, turn left into a cul-de-sac which leads to a farm. At the end of this driveway, cross the stile on your right which takes you into a field. Walk straight onwards with the edge of the field on your right. Halfway across the field turn left. The field bulges out on the left hand side. Walk up this part of the field, where there will be a small stream on your left. In the far right hand corner there is a stile which takes you onto a path through some shrubs with the stream on your left. At the end of this path you come to the road. You are now in Sutton.

Cross the road and turn right. (Take care crossing this road because it is not easy to see the traffic coming from your right.) Go straight across at the staggered cross roads. You will then come to the village hall on your right, and Symondley Road on the other side of the hall. Turn right into Symondley Road then walk to the end of the road.

Go through a small gate into a field and continue straight on across two fields. When you reach a raised bank with a small stream on the other side of it, turn right and follow the path with the stream on your left. On reaching a driveway which crosses a small bridge over the stream, go across the bridge, and then continue to follow the stream, which is now on

Sutton Reservoir

your right. This brings you out on Leek Old Road, which as its name suggests, used to be the main road to Leek before the A523 was built.

The other side of the road is Sutton Reservoir, which is known locally as Turks Head Reservoir. This is a feeder reservoir for Macclesfield canal.

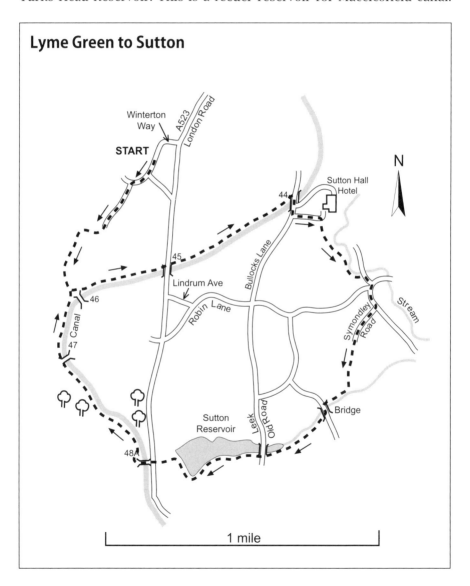

Cross the road and go through a large gate. Walk straight on, following the path, with the reservoir on your right. When you come to the far end of the reservoir, turn right and walk across the dam. At the far side, just before you reach the hedge, turn left and go down the slope, following the footpath, to London Road.

Cross the road, then cross the wooden bridge over the canal. On the canal footpath on the other side, turn under the bridge, and then continue along the footpath with the water on your right. If you now look to your right, you will see, on the other side of the water, the stone arch above the culvert which comes from the reservoir. This wooden bridge is No.48A. As you continue along the footpath you will see the stone supports where bridge No.48 used to be. Later you pass bridge No.47, which is a swing bridge to take a footpath over the canal. There is a tethered chain which can be pulled to bring this bridge over the canal. The next bridge is No.46. When you have walked under this stone arch, it is only a few yards more to the turning on your left which takes you back to the car park.

Refreshments

For lunch, try The Rising Sun on Congleton Road (A536), or the Church House Inn in Sutton. To get to the Church House Inn, drive back to London Road (A523), turn right onto it, and take the first left, Lindrum Avenue, then turn left at the T-junction, into Robin Lane. Go straight on at the cross roads, then straight on again at the staggered cross roads in Sutton. At the next junction, The Church House Inn is on your right.

Rising Sun, Congleton Road, Macclesfield SK11 7XD
The Church House Inn, Church Lane, Sutton Lane Ends, Macclesfield SK11 0DS

6. Marton

Marton is a Cheshire village on the A34, 5 miles southwest of Macclesfield. You can park in the square, which is just off the road. There are shops on three sides of the square. These include a village shop selling farm produce, incorporating a bakery selling homemade pies and cakes. There is a coffee shop and brasserie. There is also the Church Farm wishing well. Alongside the square is Marton church, which was founded in 1343, and is the oldest half-timbered church in use in Europe. It is well worth a look. It attracts visitors from many countries. Across the road from the square is the Davenport Arms where you can get a drink, or lunch, after the walk.

Distance	4 miles
Allow	2 hours
Terrain	This is an all seasons walk.
By car	In Macclesfield, drive to Broken Cross roundabout, where you turn left into Gawsworth Road then after a few yards turn right into Pexhill Road. Go straight on until you come to the T-junction with the A34. Turn left then follow this road into Marton.
Map	Philip's Ordnance Survey Street Atlas Cheshire Page 133 E3

The walk

To start the walk you leave the car park in the square and turn right onto the A34. Walk past New House Farm and the entrance to the golf course at Martins Meadow, and then turn right into Oak Lane. As you leave the main road it is immediately quieter, and you can hear the birdsong now. You will reach a T-junction with Marton Primary School on your right. Turn right into School Lane. After ten minutes of walking along school lane you come to Pikelow Farm and Martin Heath Trout Pools. Immediately after this on your right is the entrance to Martin Heath Fruit Farm, which grows strawberries, raspberries, gooseberries and currents in fields on both sides of the road. Next to the fruit farm is a lane on your

Marton Church

right with a footpath sign on the corner. There is a sign here that says 'Marton Heath Kennels and Cottage'.

You turn right into this lane, leaving the tarmac road to walk on a surface of small stones. It is dry most of the year. This lane passes between fields and then through a small wood, which is filled with rhododendrons, you then pass the kennels and cottage on your left and the lane opens out into fields again. You then get a lovely view of the hills ahead of you with the radio mast marking the point of Winkle Hill. Continue past some little ponds in clumps of trees, then out into the open again and the lane leads into the farmyard of Great Tidnock Farm.

Bear slightly right across the farmyard. As soon as you come out of the farmyard, back into the lane, you turn right, into the field at the footpath sign. Follow the fence on your right until you reach the old barn then curve to the left. The panoramic views here are superb. Once you cross the

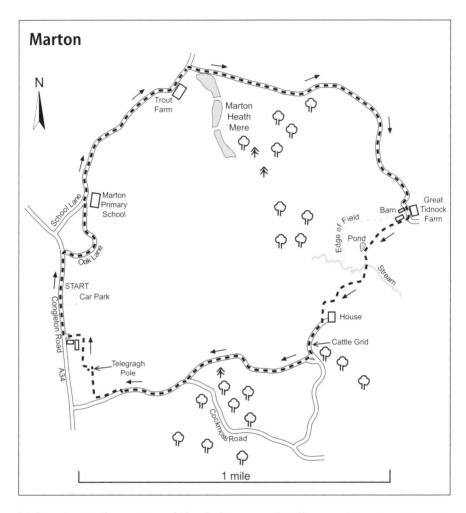

high point in the centre of the field, a pond will come into view. Pass to the left side of this pond and head straight on and you will reach a small bridge over a stream. Cross this and go straight on up the slope following a row of trees on your right.

In the top corner of the field turn right at the footpath sign, through the gate, and straight on, following the line of trees at this side of the field. At the far corner of the field the path curves to the left, following the hedge and fence on your right. At the top corner of the field there is a house straight ahead, turn right at the footpath sign into the next field, then after a few yards turn left out of it. Continue straight on, with the hedge of the house on your left. You will reach the driveway that leads to the house.

Turn right onto the drive and then follow the drive. After a short distance, when you reach a cattle grid, turn right onto a track which has trees on your right and a field on your left. Enjoy the view of the lovely skyline of hills on your left. This track has a surface of small stones, making it dry underfoot. The track leads into the farmyard of Mutlow Farm.

Continue straight on between the farm buildings on both sides. As you leave the farmyard you pass a duck pond on your left then come back onto a tarmac drive, which leads to the road. Turn right onto the road.

The Old Rectory buildings will be on your left, and opposite the end of these, there is a stile on your right.

Great Tidnock Farm

Cross the stile into the field, turn left and follow the hedge which runs alongside the road until you reach a farm gate. Turn right here and then cross this end of the field. Head straight towards a telegraph pole on the corner, then walk straight on with the hedge on your left.

You can now see Marton Church again. Keep following the hedge on your left to the far corner, where you cross a stile and turn left. Keep the hedge, and then Brookside cottage on your left until you turn left through a gate. This brings you onto the drive that leads to the cottage. Turn right and go down the drive to the road. At the road you go through a gate and turn right onto the A34. It is a busy road and noisy, with the traffic, but there is a pavement on this side, so you are quite safe, and it only takes a few minutes to walk back to Marton.

Refreshments
You can have lunch at the Davenport Arms in Marton.

Davenport Arms, Congleton Road, Marton, Macclesfield SK11 9HF

7. Peover

The gardens of Peover Hall are worth seeing, and they are open to the public at certain times if you wish to return to visit them. The parkland of Peover Hall, and its pretty river with overhanging willow trees, makes this a delightful walk.

Distance	4½ miles
Allow	2¼ hours
Terrain	There is a lovely display of snowdrops on this walk from February to mid-March, and you can also see crocus at this time.
By car	From Broken Cross at Macclesfield take the A537, which goes to Chelford and Knutsford. Just after Chelford, turn left into Pepper Street. This is signposted as going to Snelson. (Before you turn you will see the Egerton Arms just ahead on your right.) Go straight on past the first crossroads. At the second crossroads there is a war memorial on your left, and a small primary school on your right. Turn right at this crossroads then park in the lay-by on your left. If you intend to have lunch at the Olde Parkgate Inn, continue on a little further and park in the pub car park on your right.
Map	Philip's Ordnance Survey Street Atlas Cheshire Page 108 A4

The walk

Walk in the same direction as you were driving. When the road bends to the right there are two lanes that come off the bend on the left: the first is Grotto Lane; take the second one, which is unnamed. A little way down, this has a large electronically operated gate across it with a stile alongside. Cross the stile and go straight on, along a path several yards wide. Pass some houses on your right and look to your left to see the carved animals

Peover

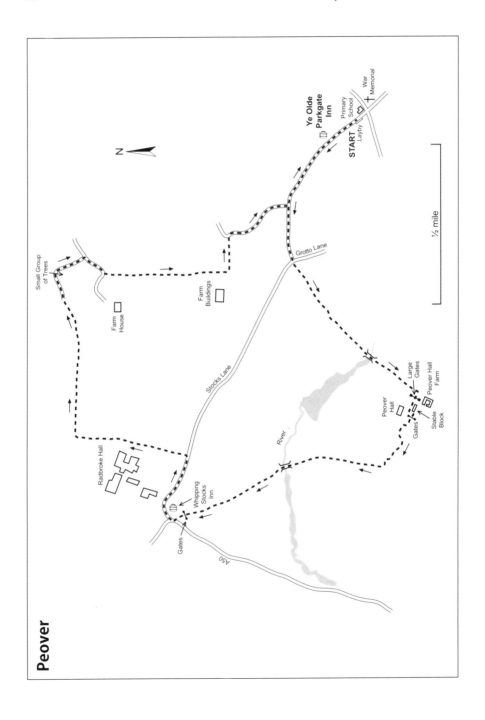

and the tree house. Go through a gate into a wide tree lined grassy avenue. As you walk along this path you will see gaps in the fences either side of you, which are filled with large tree trunks. This is where horses are used for eventing. At the end of this tree lined avenue, go through a gate, then between two ponds, over a bridge made of sleepers, into a large field.

Walk straight across this field. On your right you will see a circular low stone wall, surrounded by four very tall, old poplar trees. Did this used to be a well for Peover Hall? You will see Peover Hall on your right as you cross this field. Head straight towards the stable

Carved horse and dogs in Stocks Lane

blocks ahead of you. When you reach them, cross a stile out of this field and turn right towards the hall. Pass through large ornate metal gates and follow the path, keeping the stable block on your left. At the end of the stable block, when you reach the stepped mounting block, turn left and through another ornate set of metal gates, then turn right onto a driveway.

You will pass a wooden horse in a large cage, where riding can be taught. Next you pass the family's dog cemetery on the left, then the hall's chapel on the right. Look out for the unusual sun dial on the wall. Next the path goes past the walled garden, then through the gardens. You will then cross a stile into the corner of a field and then turn right and cross another stile. Turn left then cross another stile.

Go straight on across the next field and then cross a stile next to two wooden poles across the path, through a small wood, and over another stile, which takes you out of the small wood. Continue straight on until you reach a stile on your right. Cross this then turn left onto a path so that you are still going in the same direction. Continue down to the river. Cross

Horses grazing in Peover Hall grounds

this by way of the cattle grid – an interesting bridge, where you can see the water passing underneath. This takes you onto a wide tree lined driveway which leads up to the large gates where you exit the Peover Hall parkland.

When you pass through the gates you come out on a sharp bend in the A50. Turn right onto Stocks Lane, with the Whipping Stocks Pub on your right. Cross the road to the pavement on the other side, where the pavement is hidden behind a hedge, which is planted on the verge. Continue on until you have passed the driveway into the entrance to Barclay's Radbroke Hall then turn left immediately after the Hall's grounds.

Follow this path with Radbroke Hall on your left and a field on your right until you come to a stile on your left. Cross it and turn right, following the path through Radbroke Hall's grounds until you reach another stile on your right. Cross this then go straight across the field following the line of the hedge on your right. Go through a gap in the hedge into the next field. Turn right then after a few yards turn left. Follow the path straight across this large field which will then take you into a wide path on the other side. This path starts by having a hedge on the right, and then a little way down it has hedges both sides. It then becomes a bridle path, which leads to a T-junction with a tarmac lane. You have to turn right here.

This tarmac lane leads to the farmhouse. Before the farmhouse, turn left onto a tarmac lane which leads to farm outbuildings. Just before the buildings you have to turn left again, onto a footpath. Continue on this path straight across the field towards a hedge on the far side. When you reach the hedge cross a stile and turn right. Follow the wide bridle path between two hedges until you reach the road. At the road turn left, then continue on back to your car.

Refreshments

You can have an excellent lunch in Ye Olde Parkgate Inn, or if you drive back to the crossroads with the school and war memorial, and drive straight on, you will come to The Dog – another excellent lunch venue.

The Dog Inn, Wellbank Lane, Over Peover, Knutsford WA16 8UP
Ye Olde Parkgate Inn, Stocks Lane, Over Peover, Knutsford WA16 8TU

8. Rudyard Miniature Train Station

On this walk you can enjoy the beauty and peaceful serenity of Rudyard Lake. Also, if you enjoy water gardens, you will enjoy seeing the water that runs alongside most of the walk, but in mid-summer the grass and nettles grow tall and obscure the waterways, so it is best walked at other times of the year. In the spring, look out for the white wood-sorrel flowers and the yellow celandine and marsh marigolds.

The Rudyard Lake Steam Railway runs from the train station, along the side of Rudyard Lake. The trains run mostly at weekends, on bank holidays and in school holidays. If you would like a ride on the train, the timetables are available at the train station.

Distance	3 miles
Allow	1 hour 25 minutes
Terrain	This walk should be avoided in summer, when it becomes so overgrown that you cannot see the waterways, so it loses all its charm. This walk is very dry underfoot. Most of the paths have a surface of small stones. It is also mostly sheltered from the wind. There are very few stiles, and those that are there are very low and easy.
By car	From Macclesfield, take the A523 towards Leek. Go straight across Bosley crossroads, through Rushton Spencer, and then take a right turn into Rudyard onto Rudyard Road, the B5331. When you go under the railway bridge, turn left immediately, and go up the one-way drive into the car park of the miniature railway.
Map	Philip's Ordnance Survey Street Atlas Staffs Page 18 F8

The walk

Heading away from the road, go through the gate at the far end of the car park and straight on. This is the route of the old dismantled railway which

Rudyard Lake Steam Train station

used to run along the side of Rudyard Lake. Keep walking straight on for quite a while. The first bridge you will cross has a low metal structure in the centre, which you can pass on the right or the left. When you reach the second bridge, which has metal trellis sides, do not cross this bridge. Either turn right immediately before the bridge, down a short steep slope (be careful of loose stones underfoot making it slippery), then over a stile into a field, or turn left just before the bridge, down a slope then turn right and walk under the bridge. Either route brings you to the same place.

Walk straight on, keeping the edge of this field on your left side. There is a water course at the side of the field. Follow this and it takes you to the corner of the field diagonally opposite to where you came in. Cross the stile into the next field. Go straight across, keeping the edge of the field on your left. At the other side of the field this path will enter a lane.

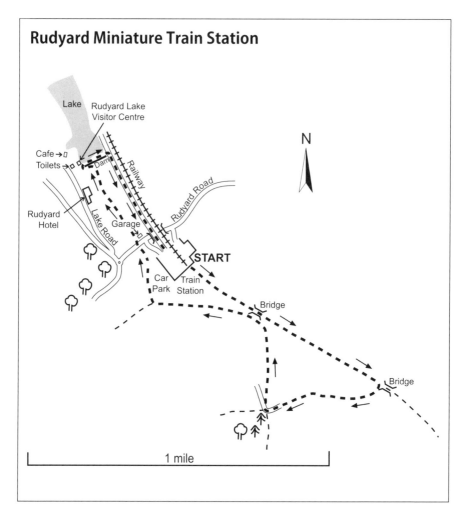

Rudyard Miniature Train Station

Continue straight on. After a few yards this lane will take a right-hand turn. There is footpath on the left and another footpath which goes straight on up a slope. This footpath leads to the churchyard at Horton where there is a gravestone for a lady who lived to be 116 years old. But we will follow the lane to the right. After a few yards it forks. The lane goes on the left fork. Take the right fork, which crosses a stile then continues on as a footpath. The path continues on straight for quite a while, following a watercourse. There are several stiles to cross while following this footpath. After a while you will see, on your right-hand side, the arch of a bridge, which is the first bridge you crossed after leaving the car park.

A little later the path which goes straight on will cross the water on a small bridge then it goes over a stile into a field. You do not take this path; you turn right. Continue to follow this path and then eventually the path brings you to the road. This is Rudyard Road, just a little further on from where you turned into the car park. Go straight across the road. There is a garage on your right. Go over the stile on the left side of the garage, and then continue along the footpath. This footpath is wider than the one you were on previously, and has watercourses running along both of its sides. Continue on until the path curves sharply left. Do not go on the path which goes straight on. Your path crosses over the watercourse, and then goes steeply uphill, turning right just at the end. It comes out at Rudyard Lake.

There is a visitor centre here, and a café and toilets, should you need them. Turn right and go across the dam, enjoying the views of the lake on

Turning the train engine for the return journey

your left. At the other side turn right again, onto the main path, which crosses the road and brings you back into the car park.

Refreshments

You can get a very nice lunch at the Rudyard Hotel. From the miniature train station, go down the one-way exit drive to the road and turn left. At the mini-roundabout turn right. Just after the mini-roundabout there is a fork, take the road on the right. After a short distance the Rudyard Hotel is on your right.

Alternatively, you could enjoy the old world charm of lunch at the Knot Inn at Rushton Spencer. From the miniature train station, go down the one-way exit drive to the road and turn right. When you reach the main road from Macclesfield to Leek, turn left. When you reach Rushton Spencer turn left into Station Lane. The Knot Inn is on your left.

Alternate parking

If you intend having lunch at The Rudyard Hotel, you can park there, by arrangement with the staff, and start the walk from there.

Knot Inn, Station Lane, Rushton Spencer, Nr Macclesfield, SK11 0QU
Rudyard Hotel, Lake Road, Rudyard, Leek, Staffordshire AT13 8RN

9. Macclesfield

This walk starts in Macclesfield town centre. At the beginning you walk alongside the river Bollin which flows through Macclesfield. Although you can start at any convenient point in town, this description starts from Tescos, which is at the side of the Bollin. If you wish to park in their car park while you walk, do check with them first, then park at the furthest end from the store so as not to prevent shoppers from parking nearer.

The walk goes across a 'snail bridge' on the canal. These bridges were designed to take the horses that pulled the boats from a footpath on one side of the canal to a footpath on the other side. Sometimes, because of the lay of the land, it was necessary to change the footpath to the other side of the canal. These bridges are unique to Macclesfield canal, and people travel here to see them.

Distance	4¼ miles
Allow	2 hours 10 minutes
Terrain	This walk is very dry underfoot, so is suitable when the weather has recently been wet and other walks may be muddy.
By car	Tescos is situated in Macclesfield at the roundabout where the Silk Road (A523) is crossed by Hibel Road (A537) and Hurdsfield Road (B5470). The access into Tescos is from Hurdsfield Road.
Map	Philip's Ordnance Survey Street Atlas Cheshire Page 87 E1

The walk

Opposite Tescos there are steps leading down to the Bollin. Walk alongside the river with the river on your right. When the path forks, take the right fork. Go through a tunnel, which passes under the Silk Road. You will then cross the Bollin and leave it behind as you walk ahead, following the paved path. Continue on this path following the Silk Road, which is on your right, until you reach Brocklehurst Way. There is a green

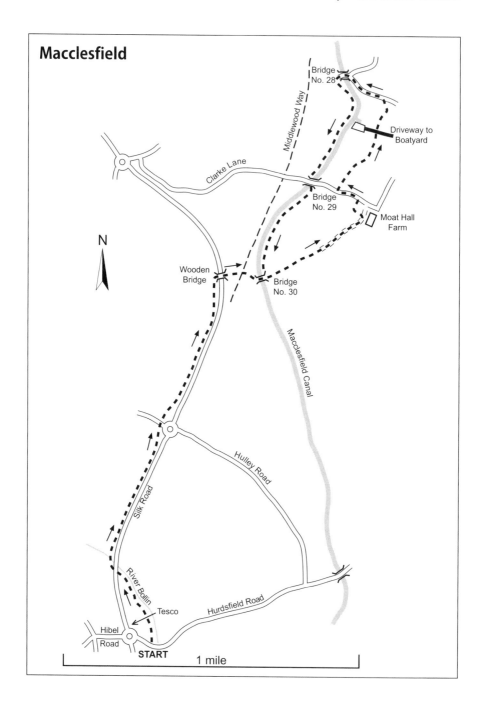

A boat breaking the ice on Macclesfield canal

man crossing to help you to cross this road safely. Go straight ahead until the path you are on turns right.

You then cross the Silk Road by way of a wooden bridge and go down the steps at the other side to where the path forks. The left fork is the Middlewood Way, which goes to Bollington. Take the right fork, which leads up to Macclesfield canal. Cross the canal across bridge number 30. Go straight on, along a path which is fenced on both sides. The path goes through a farmyard, down the farm drive, and comes out on Clarke lane. (Alternatively, you can turn left over a stile into a field before you reach Clarke Lane, and then head to the right. When you reach a stile, cross it into Clarke Lane a little lower down.)

Turn left. After about five minutes you will see a stile on your right. Cross that and go straight on across the fields. When you come to what looks like a lane – it is just the driveway to the boatyard on your left – go straight across it and straight on across the next field. When you come to the next lane, turn left on to it.

Sun and snow in January

At the fork keep left. You will then cross over the canal and effectively turn left, although the path over the bridge turns right, then by keeping turning right you go under the bridge you had just crossed. This is bridge number 28. Follow the canal path. If the water is on your left, you are going in the right direction. The next bridge, number 29, is a snail bridge. By following the path, you will cross to the other side of the canal.

The water will now be on your right. Continue on to the next bridge which is number 30. To turn right here, you cross the bridge.

From here you retrace your path, going over the same route you took on your way out.

Refreshments

You can get a very good pub lunch at several of the pubs in Macclesfield. Among others, there is The Rising Sun on Congleton Road, or the Flower Pot at the crossroads where Park lane, Ivy lane, Oxford Road and Congleton Road meet.

Rising Sun, Congleton Road, Macclesfield SK11 7XD
Flower Pot, 1 Congleton Road, Macclesfield SK11 7UF

10. Poynton Lake

You can enjoy good views on this walk. Several of the paths used to have narrow gauge railways to take the coal out, when there were coal mines in the Poynton area. These wide paths, which are tree lined and firm underfoot, are a pleasure to walk on because when you walk with friends you can walk beside each other and chat as you go. There is no need to walk in single file in the way you do on narrow paths. Also, they are an interesting remnant of Poynton's past. Poynton Lake is also known locally as Poynton Pool.

Distance	4¼ miles
Allow	2 hours 10 minutes
Terrain	This is an all year round walk.
By car	From Macclesfield take the Silk Road (A523) northwards. When you reach the cross roads in the centre of Poynton, go straight ahead then take the third turning on the right, which is South Park Drive. (Do not count the turning into the sports ground.) Pass the lake on your left. A little further on, turn left into a small car park. This is opposite Lakeside Drive.
Map	Philip's Ordnance Survey Street Atlas Cheshire Page 36 C3

The walk

On the other side of the car park is a small gate. Go through the gate and turn right. Walk in the same direction as South Park Drive, to the other side of the field, where you pass through a gate on your right back into South Park Drive. Turn left and continue along South Park Drive. Go past Anglesey Drive on your left. When you reach a T-junction with an unadopted road, turn right. This is Towers Road. A few yards further on is a gate on your left, go through the gate and then follow the wide path which goes slightly to the left across the field. At the other side you come to a gate onto a narrow road with another gate on the opposite side of the road. Go straight across.

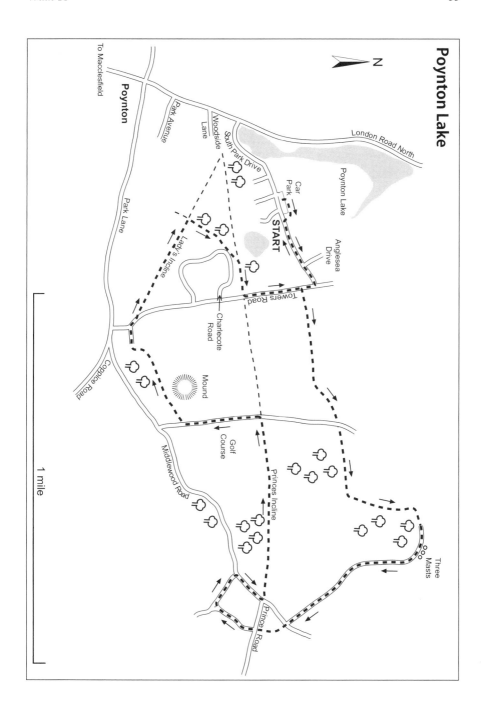

Follow the path straight on. It winds through some bushes, then at a small clump of bushes and trees on your right, behind a barbed wire fence, turn left and follow the wide path up the hill. Once you have gained a little height, you can admire the extensive view on your left, where the whole of the Cheshire plain is laid out before you. Next, you will pass a small clump of trees on your right. The path curves to the right, round these trees. Just after that, at the top of the hill, go through a gate, and then walk along an unsurfaced lane.

Walk past three large masts on your left (which may be for mobile phones, TV or radio), and continue on. A lovely panoramic view of the range of hills in the distance opens up before you. You can enjoy this as you walk, until the lane starts to go downhill, and gradually the view is lost to you.

At the end of the lane you reach Middlewood Road. Go straight across (carefully – because it is difficult to see the traffic in either direction – the

Poynton Lake

first person across can tell the others when it is safe to cross.) Go through the gate on the other side of the road and then continue straight on, on a tarmac footpath, with horse stables and a small horses' paddock on your right. You will reach a crossroads with a small lane. Go straight on, which will bring you to T-junction with a road. There is a small patch of trees in the middle of this junction. Turn right here. A short distance down this road you will come to a T-junction with Middlewood Road. There is a bus stop and bus shelter on this corner. Turn right into Middlewood Road.

There is a wide grass verge on this side of Middlewood Road. After a few minutes you will have to cross the road. This is where one of the wide footpaths, that used to have the narrow gauge railway line, crosses the road. This is called Prince's Incline. When you have crossed Middlewood Road, you will see this footpath on the left, with a private drive leading to Bluebell Rise, to the right of it. Take the footpath.

After a while, you will come to the place where a lane crosses Prince's Incline. At this point you can see the golf course on your left. Go through a gate onto this lane. Opposite, there is an unusual, funnel shaped stile. Turn left onto the lane. As you walk along this lane you will see that the golf course is on both sides of it.

You come to a large stone gatepost standing alone on your right, and a small gate behind it, turn right and go through the gate. There is a sign in front of you which says Davenport Golf Club. The fairway is on your right, and the golf tee on your left. If golfers are teeing off, you may need to wait for them, unless they wave you on. Walk straight across the fairway then through the small gate opposite. Follow the path through a small patch of trees. There is a large mound on your right. The path then curves to the left and goes up a short slope. At the top of the slope you leave the trees behind, and reach a fence, where you turn right. Continue straight on. The path then goes downhill for a while. At the bottom of this path, cross a stile beside a gate, then go on down the lane to reach Towers Road.

Turn right, then cross the road. On the other side another wide path forks off on the left of the road. This is called Lady's Incline. Go through a small gate onto this wide path and then continue straight on for a while. Next you will see a housing estate on your right. At the end of this estate you will come to a place where paths go off on both the right and the left of your wide path. Take the path on the right. This is a narrow tarmaced path, with houses behind fence panels on your right, and on your left is a wire mesh fence with a small wood behind it. Continue along here and you will soon come to the place where the curve of Charlecote Road will be on your right. But you walk straight on, staying on your path. It then comes to a T-junction with one of those wide paths. This one is Prince's Incline. Turn right onto the wide path. Continue until you cross a stile by a gate, onto the unadopted road, Towers Road, once more. Turn left onto it, then continue on until you reach South Park Drive on your left, which takes you back to your car.

Refreshments

For lunch drive back down South Park Drive to the main road, turn left towards Macclesfield, then go straight across at the cross roads. Shortly afterwards The Vernon Arms is on your left, where you can get a pub lunch. Or if you continue straight on, until you reach the traffic lights at Adlington, The Legh Arms, which has a carvery, is on your left

Legh Arms, London Road, Adlington, Macclesfield SK10 4NA
Vernon Arms, London Road South, Poynton, Stockport SK12 1LQ

11. Redesmere and Capesthorne Hall Lakes

On this walk you can enjoy the beauty of the lakes at Redesmere and Capesthorne. You can see a wide variety of wildfowl at Redesmere. There is an information board to help to identify the species. Or you can just take some bread to feed the ducks.

Distance	**3½ miles**
Allow	**1¾ hours**
Terrain	**This can be made into a shorter walk by turning left when you reach Mill Lane, and then turn right onto Congleton Road.**
By car	**In Macclesfield, take the road to Broken Cross (A537). At the roundabout turn left into Gawsworth Road, then after a few yards turn right into Pexhill Road (B5392). After three and a half miles you come to the A34. Turn right then take the first turning on your right, which is Redesmere Lane. Park next to the lake.**
Map	**Philip's Ordnance Survey Street Atlas Cheshire Page 110 A2**

The walk

When you leave the car, walk with Redesmere on your left. About 100 yards up the road you come to a stile on your left. Cross this and walk straight on over a small field, then over another stile. Continue along a fenced path, and then follow the path straight on, through trees until you cross a stile and leave the wood. This brings you onto a wider path with a surface of stones. Pass the boats in the boatyard on your left, then a little more of the lake on your left, then turn left and through a stile which takes you into a small wood at the end of the lake. After passing the outflow of the lake you reach the main road. This is the A34.

Go straight across the road and over another stile. Go straight on, with the side of the field on your right, until you reach the lake at Capesthorne.

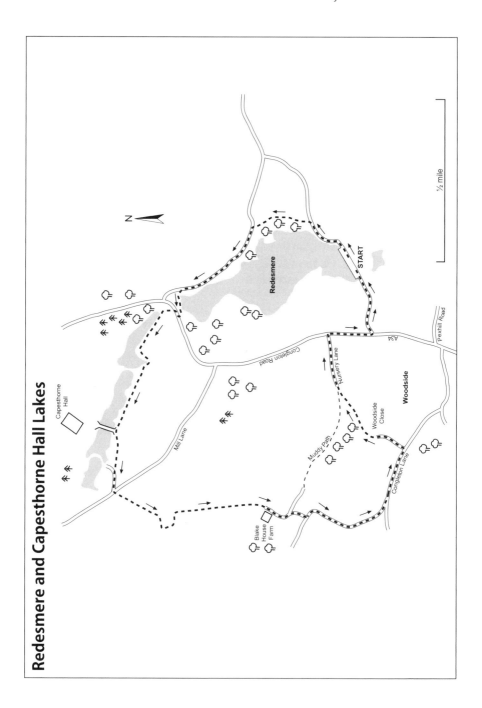

Redesmere and Capesthorne Hall Lakes

Duck feeding station at Redesmere

Turn left. After a few yards, cross a stile then turn right. Continue straight on, with the Capesthorne lakes on your right, until you reach a road.

Go straight across the road and over another stile, then straight on across a field. Go over another stile then through a farm gate. A few yards further on, cross another stile, then turn left and go straight across this field to the next stile. After the next field the footpath forks off on the left – it is marked with a yellow footpath arrow. This brings you through a farm gate, across a farm track and then through a second farm gate into the farm yard. Continue straight on, out of the farm. At the crossroads, go straight on. You come to a T-junction, where you turn left. This brings you out on to Congleton Lane. You turn left onto this road.

After a short distance you pass a signpost that shows that you are walking towards Siddington. You will have to follow this road for about 10 minutes, but it is a quiet road, with little traffic. When you come to a road

Looking across Capesthorne lakes to Capesthorne Hall

called Woodside on your left, turn into it. At the end of Woodside there is a road on the left called Woodside Close. Go to the end of Woodside Close, where there is a path to the left side of the end of the close. Turn onto this path, keeping to the left. Follow the well defined path which has a row of bushes on its left side. This path brings you into Nursery lane. Go straight on to the A34 where you turn right, then after a short distance, turn left into Redesmere Lane, and back to your car.

Refreshments

Take the A34 north to Monks Heath crossroads. Turn right at the traffic lights onto the A537 heading towards Macclesfield. At Henbury you will reach The Blacksmiths Arms on your right, and a little further on, The Cock, also on your right. Both offer excellent lunches.

Blacksmiths Arms, Chelford Road, Henbury, Macclesfield SK11 9PG
The Cock, Chelford Road, Henbury, Macclesfield SK10 3LH

12. Astbury Mere

Asbury mere is very picturesque, with a wildflower meadow that is at its best in the spring. The paths on this walk are mostly wide, so that you can chat to your companions as you walk, and a lot of it is shaded, making it is a suitable walk for hot sunny days.

The section of the canal that you walk along is very beautiful: the houses which back onto the canal have lovely gardens which come right down to the water, where they have little landing stages. The narrow boats which travel up and down are very picturesque. The bridge you pass is a unique 'Snail Bridge' which was used in the past to take the horses which pulled the barges, to the other side of the canal.

Part of this walk follows 'The Priestly Trail'. In the past it was not possible for both Astbury and Congleton to have a priest, so one priest had to serve both. The Priestly Trail was the route he regularly walked.

Distance	3¼ miles
Allow	1 hour 40 minutes
Terrain	There are no stiles on this walk, but there are quite a few steps. The footpaths stay dry. Early in June you can see the wild orchids in the wildflower meadow. Later in June the yellow iris are in flower by the canal.
By car	From Macclesfield take the road to Congleton. This will join the A34 just before you reach Congleton. Stay on the A34 until you are leaving Congleton. Just after the 2nd roundabout turn left into Sandy Lane. There is a brown sign pointing down this road which says 'Asbury Mere Country Park'. Go to the end of Sandy Lane and into the car park.
Map	Philip's Ordnance Survey Street Atlas Cheshire Page 156 A1

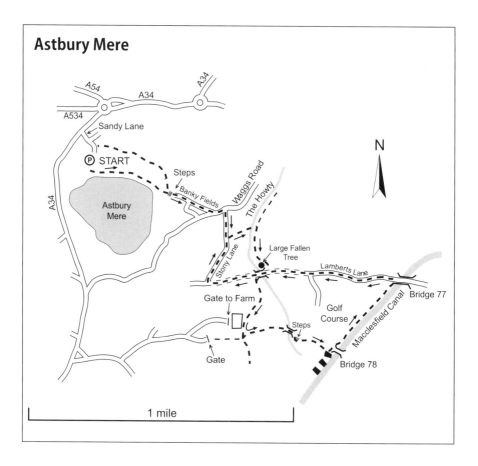

Astbury Mere

The walk

Walk along the path with the mere on your right. There are two paths going in this direction. If you take the higher one, you will get a better view of the mere and surrounding countryside and the hills beyond. You will also pass alongside the wild flower meadow. If you take the lower path you will be able to see the water fowl and swans on the lake. Both paths join up again into a single path.

When your path divides take the left turning, go up a short slope, then go up 15 steps. These steps are not very high, and are wide, so they are easy to climb. Then turn right and there are another 26 steps to climb. This gets most of the steps of this walk over with while you are still fresh. At the top of the steps a path goes straight across; turn left onto it and then continue straight on. The path joins a road called Bankyfields. At the end of this road it forms a T-junction with Waggs Road. Turn left. After a few yards turn right into a narrow lane called Stony Lane. There is a signpost pointing down this lane which says 'Astbury village.'

Walk along here for a short distance until you come to an opening on your left where you go down a short steep slope and through a small gate. The gate is labelled 'Priestly Trail.' '(If you wish to avoid the short steep slope, continue past it for 100 yards, then double back on yourself on a path that takes you to the bottom of the slope.)Continue straight on and through another gate labelled the same, then you will come to a place where the footpath goes over a wide bridge which crosses a stream called 'The Howty'.

When you have crossed the bridge turn right and head up the slope. The path follows the direction of the stream, but there is a steep slope from

Astbury Mere

your path to the stream below. You then enter a gate and the next part of the path has trees along both sides of it. At the end of this section go through a gate into Lambert Lane. There is a signpost in front of you with the name on it. Turn right here.

Walk along a few yards and then you will come to the Howty again. The path divides and both parts go over little bridges which cross the stream. The path on the right goes round a large tree which is bent over the path. You will come back to this later. For now, go straight on, over the little bridge and through the small gate into the field. Bear slightly left across the field to the next small gate. Continue straight on, following the path, through two more fields. You then go over a footbridge which crosses a stream, and then up 22 steps.

This brings you out onto the fairway of a golf course. Straight ahead of you, you will see a small wood. Cross the fairway and enter the wood. Follow the footpath through the wood. This will bring you out onto the canal at the point where a footbridge, which is number 78, crosses the canal. Turn left and walk along the towpath with the water on your right.

Snail bridge

This is a beautiful section of the canal. The towpath of this section is wide, enabling you to walk beside your companions, and not in single file like most towpaths. The gardens on the other side are very pretty, and come right down to the water. The next bridge you come to, number 77, is a 'snail bridge'. Turn left just before the bridge and go up the steps. At the top there is a signpost telling you that the road which crosses the bridge is called 'Lambert Lane'. Turn left onto Lambert Lane.

After a short while you will come to the junction where you first came onto Lambert Lane. But this time take the turning on the right. Cross over the little stream and then you will immediately pass a very large bent tree on your right which forces the path to go around it. Continue straight on along a fenced path. At the end of this fenced path you go through a gate onto the end of Stony Lane. There is a junction of five paths here. Straight ahead is a pair of large iron gates, with some old farm buildings on the other side of them. On the right of these is a footpath. There is also a footpath on the left of these gates, this one is labelled 'priestly trail'. But the one you want is the sharp right turn onto Stony Lane. This is also labelled 'priestly trail'. Initially this almost doubles back on the direction in which you have just come, but then it curves round to the left, and goes uphill.

Stony Lane will bring you back to Waggs Road again, but just before that, you will pass, on your right, the place where you turned down at the start. At Waggs Road turn left, then right into Bankyfields, and straight on to the top of the steps that take you back to Astbury Mere. Retrace your steps back to your car.

Refreshments

You can have a very good lunch at the Cheshire Tavern. Drive back to the A34 and turn right. At the second roundabout turn left into Obelisk Way, then turn left into the Cheshire Tavern.

Cheshire Tavern, West Road, Congleton CW12 4EY

13. Jodrell Bank

This is a delightful walk with a variety of scenery. In the spring you can look out for the wood sorrel, wood anemone and stichwort along the way. There are woods full of bluebells and near the end of the walk there is a beautiful natural bank of primroses.

On this walk you will be able to see the large dish of the Lovell Telescope, which is the main telescope of the Jodrell Bank Radio Astronomy Observatory. It is the third largest steerable radio telescope in the world.

Distance	**4 miles**
Allow	**2 hours**
Terrain	Look out for the primroses on this walk in mid-April, and for the wood anemone carpeting the woods on the first quarter of the walk.
By car	From Macclesfield, take the A537 towards Knutsford. Go straight on at the traffic lights at Monks Heath. When you come to the Chelford roundabout turn left onto the A535. After about 5 minutes you come to a brown sign on your left which points to the road on your right, and says 'Jodrell Bank.' The main road turns sharp left here. Take the right turn, into Bomish Lane. Go past the entrance to Jodrell Bank on your left, over a narrow bridge which crosses the railway, and you will then come to a black and white house at a fork in the road. Turn right here, taking care because it is difficult to see traffic coming from the left. Pass the 1st lay-by on your left, because it is very small, and then park in either the 2nd lay-by, or in the 3rd one, which is a little further up the lane.
Map	Philip's Ordnance Survey Street Atlas Cheshire Page 108 A2

The walk

Start walking in the same direction as you were driving. When you reach the T-junction, turn right. Immediately afterwards there is a footpath on your left, which forks off from the road. Go down this path. It goes through a lovely wood. When the path comes out of the woods and you can see a building of Woodend Farm up ahead, look for a stile and a signpost on your right. The sign will say 'Peover Superior Church 1 mile'. Turn right, go over the stile, then straight on across the field.

At the other side cross another stile into woods again. Go along this path, which then goes down a set of steps. At the bottom there is a small brook, which is the Peover Eye. There are two footbridges crossing this stream, the one on the left is very narrow and the one on the right is slightly wider. Cross the water, then go up another set of steps on the other side. At the top go over a stile into a field, then go straight on, following the fence on your right. When the fence turns away from you, turn to your right and follow it. After about 100 yards, you will see two stiles on your left. They both converge onto the same path in the woods. Turn towards either stile, cross it, and

Old type stile at Peover

then follow the path in the woods. This path will take you over another bridge which crosses another branch of the Peover Eye. As soon as you have crossed the bridge, turn right, then after a few yards turn left and go uphill through the woods.

At the top, go over a stile into a field. Turn immediately right to follow the fence on your right, to the corner, then turn left, and continue to follow the fence at the edge of the field.

When you cross a stile next to a gate, onto the road, turn right. You will pass two driveways together on your left. The one on the left leads to

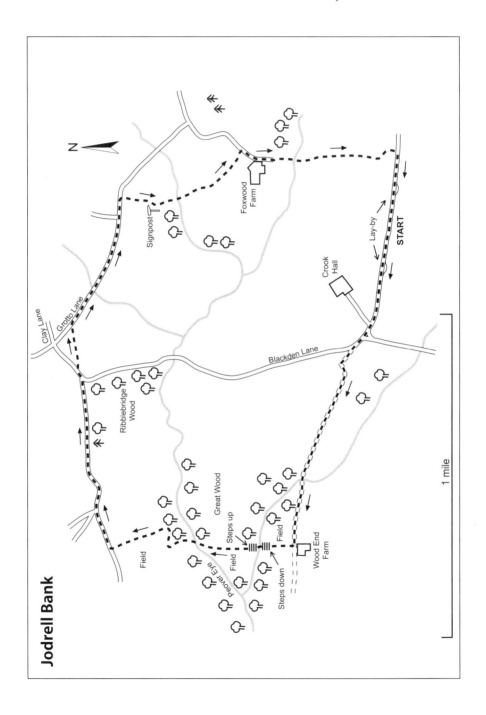

Jodrell Bank

Peover Hall Farm and the one on the right leads to Peover Hall. Continue on past these. You will pass through a set of white gates, then through a second set of white gates. At the second set there is a sign on the other side of them saying 'Peover Hall'.

When you come out at a T-junction with Clay Lane, turn left. After a few yards turn right, and cross a stile. Bear left to cross this field, or if it is planted, walk around the edge. Cross a stile then straight on across another smaller field. Cross another stile into Grotto Lane, and turn right. Pass several large houses on your right, and then walk with just fields on either side of the road. The last place on your right is Chaseley Farm. Then just after you go past a side road on your left, you will pass a small pond on your left, and then there will be farm gates on either side of the road.

Turn right here, cross a stile, and go straight on along the side of the field. Look out for signpost on your right, which tells you to turn left. Turn left

The Peover Eye at Foxwood Farm

at this point and go across the field, heading towards a small circular wood. When you reach it bear left, and keep its fence on your right. Cross another stile and go straight on. This brings you to a gate which leads down a short drive into the road. Turn right and follow this road into the farmyard of Foxwood Farm. On your left is a house which has a stone plaque on the front declaring it was built in 1792. Bear left round this house, then go down the sloping path, through a gate into a field. Cross the field. Go over a wide bridge across a stream, which is the Peover Eye once again, up the slope and straight on. Follow the yellow footpath marker at the next stile, which indicates that you go straight on to cross the next field. When you cross a stile into a road, turn right. You will find the lay-by where you parked on your left.

Refreshments

Continue down the road in the direction you were driving. At the T-junction turn left. At the next T-junction turn right, which takes you into Goostrey. Then at the next T-junction turn left. You will find the Red Lion on your left. They serve an excellent lunch here. Alternatively there is also the Crown in Goostrey, or the Olde Parkgate Inn at Peover, or The Dog at Peover.

Red Lion Inn, Station Road, Goostrey CW4 8PJ
The Crown, 111 Main Road. Goostrey CW4 8PE
Ye Olde Parkgate Inn, Stocks Lane, Over Peover, Knutsford WA16 8TU
The Dog Inn, Wellbank Lane, Over Peover, Knutsford WA16 8UP

14. Fernilee

The Goyt Valley is a local beauty spot. There are two reservoirs: there is no path round Errwood, but you can walk round Fernilee. This is a very beautiful walk. The whole area is very picturesque, not just the lake, but also the roads leading to it. It is enchanting in all seasons. In October all the trees are in shades of gold, orange, red, and yellow. It is well worth visiting then. In the summer, on a bright sunny day, the huge bank of trees that line the whole length of one side of the lake are reflected in the water. If you take a photo on a calm day you cannot tell which way up to hold the photo because of the reflections. In winter it is better not to visit because the roads leading up to the lake can be frozen and slippery.

Distance	3¾ miles
Allow	1 hour 50 minutes
Terrain	This is a walk with no stiles. On hot sunny days this walk gives quite a bit of shade. The dappled sunshine coming through the trees is very picturesque. In autumn the colours of the trees across the lake are spectacular. But this walk should be avoided in winter, when the roads to it can be icy.
By car	From Macclesfield, take Hurdsfield Road (B5470) which becomes Rainow Road and leads to Rainow. On the other side of Rainow, when you have passed the Robin Hood pub on your left, take the next road on your right, which is Smith Lane. At the T-junction turn right, then when you come to a small grassy triangle in the centre of the place where 3 roads meet, turn left and go downhill. When you come to the next T-junction, there is a small chapel on your right, called Jenkins Chapel, Salterford. Turn right here. A little further on, pass the turning on your left which leads to the Pym Chair car park, and go straight on. This road is narrow, with passing places. After 1½ miles you will come to a car park on your right and Errwood reservoir on your left. You reach the exit of the car park first, so you have to drive a little further down the road to reach the entrance.
Map	Philip's Ordnance Survey Street Atlas Cheshire Page 90 C2

Fernilee

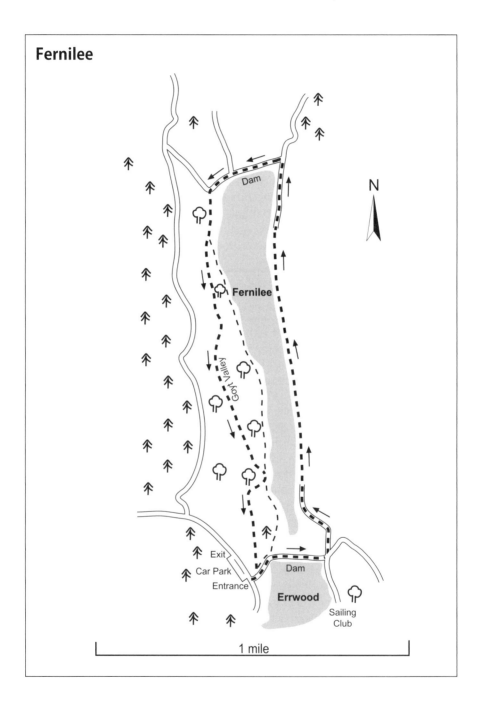

N

Dam

Fernilee

Goyt Valley

Exit

Car Park

Entrance

Dam

Errwood

Sailing
Club

1 mile

After the walk, the drive into Bollington for lunch is one of the most scenic routes in this area. You will see the folly 'White Nancy', which is Bollington's landmark, on your left on this road.

The walk

Opposite the car park is the dam of Errwood reservoir, with a road going across the dam. Errwood is on the right of this road, and Fernilee is on the left. Fernilee is lower down, so you don't see it until you are walking across the dam. You can walk either way round Fernilee. Whichever way you choose to go, there will be a steep slope down at the beginning and a steep slope up at the end.

To start, walk along the road which goes across the dam. At the other side turn left, and go down the road to the locked barrier which prevents cars from passing. Go round the barrier and down this steep road. When you reach the bottom the road becomes a path and turns right.

Continue to walk with the lake on your left. As you walk the whole length of the lake, you can enjoy the views across the water to the wooded bank on the other side. Near the other end of the lake the path becomes a road. When you reach the dam the road goes straight on, and there is also a left

The path on the west side of Fernilee crossing a gully

turning, which crosses the dam. Turn left here. There is a scenic view from the dam, looking up the lake which is used on calendars. Do stop to admire it before continuing on.

On the other side of the dam, turn left at the T-junction. A few yards further on you have a choice:

1) When you reach a gate on your left, you can walk past it and continue on the road, which turns right and goes steeply uphill to a T-junction where you turn left. You then walk the whole length of the lake along a road through woods, which takes you back to the road with the car park. Turn left and go downhill back to the car.

2) Or, if you prefer paths, go through the gate and then follow the path. When it forks, you can take the right fork. Or, you can take the left fork and follow the lakeside path.

Continue to the end of the reservoir where the path turns right and goes steeply uphill. It then joins another path which comes in from your right. Turn left onto this path. If you want to avoid the steep slope at the end, take the sloping uphill path a short distance before you reach the end of the reservoir. This brings you to the same place. Continue on and you come back to the road which crosses the dam of Errwood. Turn right onto this road to go back to the car park.

Refreshments

Bollington is the nearest place for lunch. Drive back in the direction in which you came, but when you reach Smith Lane, do not turn left into it, but go straight on, into Pike Road. When you reach the main Macclesfield Road, turn right and then immediately left, into Blaze Hill. This road meanders down into Bollington. Once you reach Bollington, turn left at the mini roundabout and go along the main road through the centre of Bollington. At the other end of Bollington, you will see the Cock and Pheasant on your right. You can have a very enjoyable lunch here.

Alternatively, turn right at the Cock and Pheasant and then continue on to the main Macclesfield road, the A523. Turn right onto this road, and then continue on the Legh Arms at the traffic lights at Adlington.

Cock and Pheasant, 15 Bollington Road, Bollington, Macclesfield SK10 5EJ
Legh Arms, London Road, Adlington, Macclesfield SK10 4NA

The sun filtering through the trees on the west side of Fernilee

15. Miners Arms at Poynton

This walk has a lot of variety, which makes it very enjoyable. There are views of the Cheshire Plain and the Pennine foot-hills.

There used to be a lot of coal mining in this area, which is the reason for the name of the pub. At the start of the walk, you can still see small pieces of coal in the path.

Distance	**3¾ miles**
Allow	**1 hour 50 minutes**
Terrain	**The yellow iris are at their best in mid-June. Look for them on the canal on the last part of the walk.**
By car	**Take the Silk Road (A523) out of Macclesfield towards Poynton. At the traffic lights at Adlington, where the Legh Arms is, go straight on. Take the first road on the right after the Legh Arms, which is Street Lane. On the left there is a signpost saying this road goes to Pott Shrigley. At the T-junction turn left. When you reach a crossroads you will see the sign for the Miners Arms on your left. Turn left, and then left into the pub car park. If you let them know that you are returning for lunch, they will not object to you parking here.**
Map	**Philip's Ordnance Survey Street Atlas Cheshire Page 63 D4**

The walk

When you walk out of the pub car park, turn left, then after a few yards, left again and over a stile. Go straight on, on a wide path, fenced on both sides, and then continue on a narrow path fenced on both sides. Go through a small gate onto a raised path across open ground. Continue to follow the path. You then go through a gate onto a wide path which is fenced on both sides. After walking down this path for a short time you will see stables to your left. You then come to a path on your left which is fenced on both sides. Turn left onto this path. Pass the stables on the

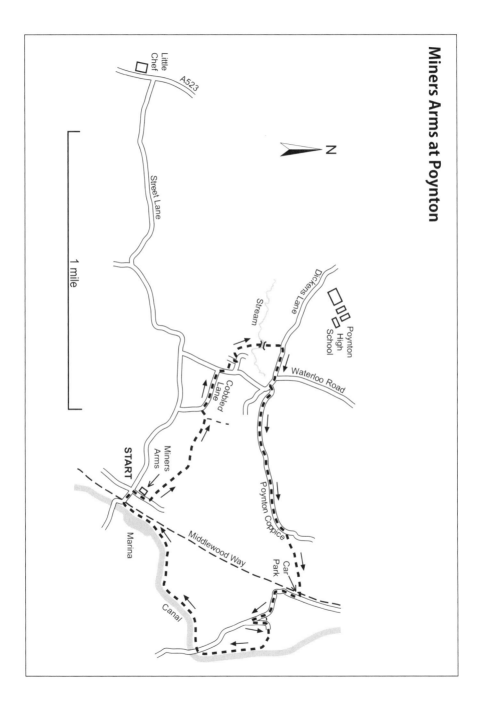

Miners Arms at Poynton

left and the ménage for horse training on the right. At the end of this path there is a gate for walkers alongside the farm gate leading to the stables. Turn right here, on to a cobbled lane.

At the end of the lane you reach the road. Turn right then immediately left, and then go through a small gate, which is marked as a footpath. This path takes you down the side of a garden. Go out of a gate at the other side, and turn right on the drive. After a few yards turn left. This leads to a car repair garage and wood workshop on your right. Opposite them on your left is a stile.

Cross the stile, go a few yards through woods, then over a stream and immediately turn right. Cross the small field, keeping the stream on your right. Go over a stile and down the side of another small field to reach a bridge, which is a few yards long, has a narrow concrete walkway and metal handrails. Cross this and go up the slope to a path, which is fenced on both sides. This leads you to Dickens Lane.

You will see Poynton High School diagonally to your left. Turn right. Cross Waterloo Road, which is on your left. You come to a lane on your left called The Coppice. Turn left into that lane. Follow it past some houses and continue uphill for 5 or 10 minutes until you go through a large gate. It is then only a short distance to where a footpath branches off on your right. Take that right fork and follow the footpath through the woods, called Poynton Coppice, until you reach the end of the path.

The Middlewood Way crosses to your right and left. On the other side of it is a small car park. On the other side of that is the road, which is parallel to the Middlewood Way.

(If you want to shorten the walk, you can turn right on to the Middlewood Way; continue until you take a right fork which is signposted to the Miners Arms, then turn right at the road.)

On reaching the Middlewood Way, turn right and walk through the car park and then turn right on to the road a little lower down. Follow the road round the bend, walking on the right so that you can see oncoming traffic coming round the bend. Just after the bend you come to Brook Bank Farm on your right. On the opposite side of the road is a stile signposted 'To the canal'. Cross this stile, go down a slope and over another stile onto a lane. Turn left and the lane immediately crosses the

A narrow boat on Macclesfield canal

brook the farm was named after. (Alternatively, if the slope is slippery due to rain, you can avoid it. Walk past the stile signposted 'To the canal' and then turn a sharp left into the lane.) Follow the lane uphill. It is paved until you reach a house on your right. After that continue straight on, but it becomes a narrower, unpaved path, which is lined with closely planted trees on both sides. After a short distance you will reach the canal.

At the canal, turn right onto the canal towpath and then follow the towpath. Go under bridge number 17, then pass a large marina full of many narrow boats, then at the next bridge, number 18, turn right off the canal. At the road turn right, then at the crossroads turn right to find the Miners Arms on your left.

Refreshments
You can have a very good lunch at the Miners Arms.

Miners Arms, Wood Lane North, Adlington, Macclesfield SK10 4PF

16. Lyme Park

The walk up from the west gate of Lyme Park is very beautiful. It follows the path of a small stream which tumbles over many small falls. The trees overhead, which shade the path, are old and well established. At the top, this path opens out into a fine vista of the Cheshire Plain.

The walk then drops down to the Middlewood Way. This is a footpath, cycleway, nature trail and bridleway, which was created out of an old derelict railway line. The line went from Macclesfield to Marple via Bollington, and was used to carry coal from the Poynton collieries until 1935.

At Higher Poynton the platform of the old station still remains. It is a picnic area now. The Nelson Pitt visitor centre, which is by the old station, will tell you more about the area's history, or visit the Anson museum in Anson Road.

'Pride and Prejudice' was filmed in Lyme Park. It was used as the house and estate of Mr. Darcy. There is information about this at the Lyme Park visitor centre.

Distance	3¾ miles
Allow	1 hour 50 minutes
Terrain	This walk stays dry underfoot. The route can be made shorter by turning left at the crossroads of paths half way round. There are lots of Bluebells on the way up to Lyme Park, in early May.
By car	Take the Silk Road (A523) out of Macclesfield towards Poynton. At the traffic lights at Adlington, by the Legh Arms, turn right. Continue straight on, passing all the roads that come off on the left, including one with a grassy triangle at its junction. When you come to a place where your road turns right, and there is a grassy triangle, turn left. Continue straight on. After a while you will go through a tunnel that passes under the canal. A short distance afterwards, the road bends sharply to the right. At the other side of this bend there is a car park on the left, next to the Middlewood Way. Park here.
Map	Philip's Ordnance Survey Street Atlas Cheshire Page 37 E2

The walk

With the Middlewood Way behind you and Shrigley Road in front, turn right. Walk round the sharp bend in the road. On the left you will find a track which comes off at a sharp angle. Walk down this track through the wood. At the bottom of the slope cross a stream, and then the track curves round to the right and goes uphill. It comes out on Macclesfield Canal. Turn right and walk with the water on your left.

The canal will cross Shrigley Road. Just before it does, go down the steps on your right. Turn left at the bottom and walk through the tunnel under the canal. After a few minutes walk along the road, following a stream on your left, you will come to a small gate at the end of a lay-by on your left. Go through the gate and up the short narrow path which continues to follow the stream. At the top it comes out onto a road. Go diagonally left to the large iron gates of West Parkgate.

Go through a small gate next to the large gates, and then walk uphill through Hase Bank Wood, following the course of a very pretty stream

Walking alongside the canal

that tumbles down over many rocks and through several little pools. It is attractive in all seasons of the year. At the top of the slope you come out at large wooden gates. Go through the small gate beside them into a car park of Lyme Park.

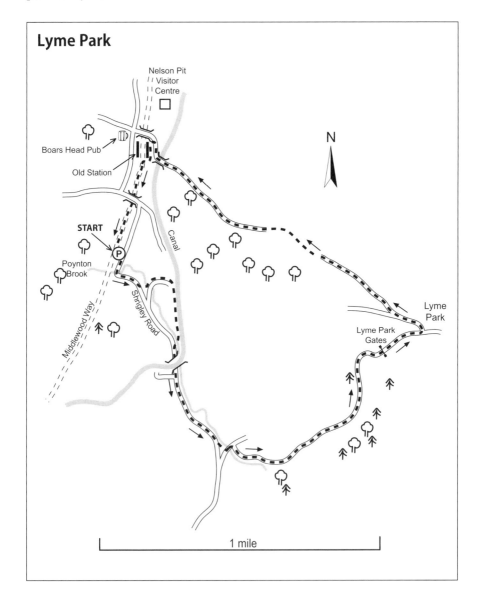

Lyme Park

The view from the bridge at Nelson Pit Visitor Centre

Go straight on, along the park driveway. Turn left onto a wide footpath that goes off at a sharp angle. (If you want to go to Lyme Park visitor centre and National Trust shop, continue straight on.) When this new footpath forks, take the right fork. You will get a fantastic view of the whole Cheshire Plain laid out before you. You can pick out all the landmarks you know, and watch the aeroplanes going in and out of Manchester Airport. Continue straight on. The path will drop down and after a while you will go out of Lyme Park. Continue straight on until reaching the canal. Cross the canal and within a few minutes you reach the Middlewood Way.

On your right is the Nelson Pit Visitor centre, where you can find out more about the local history. On the other side of the Middlewood Way is the Boar's Head pub. The road you are on continues as Anson Road, which has the Anson Engine Museum just a short way ahead.

Turn left onto the Middlewood Way. You will pass the remaining platform of the old railway station, which has now become a picnic area. Continue along the Middlewood Way until you come back to your car.

Refreshments

The Legh Arms at Adlington is a carvery which provides an excellent lunch. You passed it on your way out, so just retrace your route.

Legh Arms, London Road, Adlington, Macclesfield SK10 4NA

A family of Canada Geese and goslings

17. Gawsworth

Near the start, you walk up a slope to find a wonderful panoramic view with a backdrop of the hills in the distance. Later, the walk along Macclesfield Canal offers some beautiful picturesque scenes. The canal at this point is wider than normal, and looks more like a river.

You will also cross The Moss, which is a very curious place with an interesting history, and a strange, moody atmosphere. The trees are heavily covered in moss, and there is more water than land. It is reminiscent of a Disney film.

Peat used to be cut from The Moss for use as fuel. You can still see the remains of old sleepers which used to support the rails of the trucks that carried the peat. Some Macclesfield cottages came with a legal right to part of the peat from The Moss for their cottage fires. The Moss is now a wildlife reserve.

Distance	**4 miles**
Allow	**2 hours**
Terrain	It can be made half as long by turning left when you reach Woodhouse End Road. This is an all season walk.
By car	From Macclesfield, take Congleton Road, the A536, travelling south. At the crossroads with Church Lane on the left, turn left. Drive along Church Lane until you see a stile on the left, just before you reach Gawsworth Hall. Park at the side of the road, near the stile. You will come over this stile at the end of the walk.
Map	Philip's Ordnance Survey Street Atlas Cheshire Page 134 B4

The walk

Walk straight ahead. Go over the bridge, past the entrance to Gawsworth Hall on your right, past some more buildings on your right, then past a pond on your left. Go straight on, through a gate into a field. Continue straight on until you reach a road. Turn right onto the road. This is Woodhouse End Road.

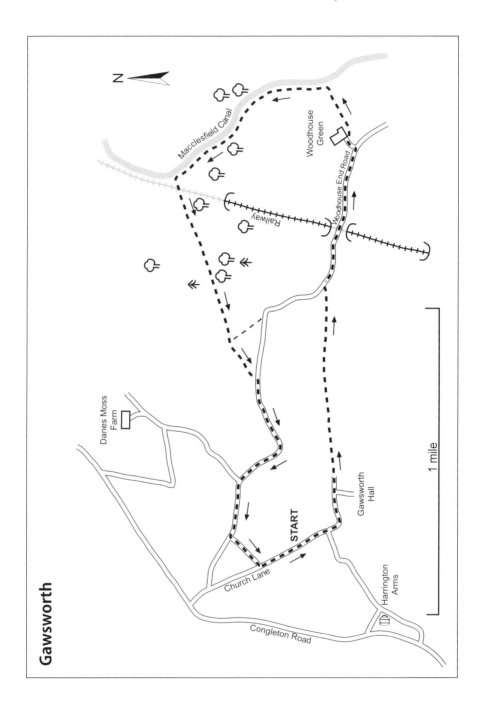

Gawsworth

Continue along this road, which crosses over the railway line, and then turn left into a lane leading to a farm called Woodhouse Green. When you reach the farmyard, turn right and enter the field. Keep to the left. After a few yards cross a stile on your left, then turn right and walk across the field. This field slopes downhill to the canal. In the middle of the field there is a stile which is not attached to anything. After the stile there is a hollow which crosses your path. In the centre is a land bridge which takes you to the other side. Walk straight ahead to a gap in the hedge and then over a stile. This takes you onto a short path which leads up to the canal.

At the canal turn left. Walk along the canal with the water on your right. Pass the lock-keepers cottage on your left, then go under footbridge number 48A. Continue on until you come to the next bridge which is number 47. This is a hand operated swing bridge, which is parked on the other side of the canal. At this point, turn left and follow the path to the railway line. Use the footbridge to cross the railway line, and then continue straight on into Danes Moss.

The frozen canal on a winter walk

In The Moss some of the ground is raised, with ditches surrounding it, to keep the land out of the water. Other parts are very boggy or under water. You will cross several bridges which go over the ditches. When you reach the other side of The Moss, there is an information board saying that this is a wildlife reserve, and giving details of the wildlife that can be seen here.

When you leave The Moss, you will come out at a cross roads of paths. Turn right. Follow the tree lined path until it leads into a field. Continue on, bearing slightly left across the field. At the other side of the field cross a stile into a driveway and then turn left. When you come to the road, which is Lowes Lane, take the road on the left. When you come to a T-junction with Woodhouse Lane, turn right. After a few minutes turn left into Wardle Crescent. This has a pavement on your right, where you walk past some beautiful gardens. On your left there are views over open countryside. After a few minutes you come to Church Lane. Turn left to return to your car.

Refreshments

Leaving Gawsworth Hall behind you head back to Congleton Road. Turn right into Congleton Road. A short way down, you will find The Rising Sun on your left, where you can enjoy an excellent lunch.

Rising Sun, Congleton Road, Macclesfield SK11 7XD

18. The River Bollin at Prestbury

This is a very pleasant walk, with plenty of variety. You start by walking along the side of the River Bollin, as it meanders along its winding way. Later on you reach a high point where you get a great view over the rolling Cheshire countryside. You will also pass a very pretty little pond where the waterfowl always raise their broods of chicks.

Distance	3¾ miles
Allow	1 hour 50 minutes
Terrain	This is an all seasons walk.
By car	From Macclesfield take the Silk Road, the A523, northwards. Turn left at the roundabout which has a road sign for Prestbury. Go along the B5091 to the T-junction, and then turn right onto Heybridge Lane. Follow this road into Prestbury village. As you enter the village, turn right into the car park.
Map	Philip's Ordnance Survey Street Atlas Cheshire Page 87 D4

The walk

On this car park both the exit and entrance are one-way for cars. Walk out of the exit, up the slope past the houses, and then turn left into Scott Road, then right into Bollin Grove. Walk to the end of this road, then continue straight on, walking on a driveway. This drive crosses the River Bollin and then goes up to Spittle House, but just before it crosses the river you will see a small gate on your right. Go through the gate and follow the path alongside the river.

The path goes through woods, then after a while it comes out into a field. Continue straight on, with the river on your left until you come to a narrow metal footbridge over the river. Cross the river and then follow the path uphill through the trees. It will curve round to the right. There is then a stile on your left. Cross this and you will find that you are on the golf course.

You may need to wait for golfers to tee off, but then continue straight on, along the right side of the fairway. Following the path, enter a small wood opposite and then follow the path through the wood until you come to a path turning off on your left. This will bring you out of the wood. Turn right and then follow the path which will go straight across the fairway.

A right turn will take you past the farm buildings of Woodside Farm. When you reach the lane which joins the farm to the main road, turn left.

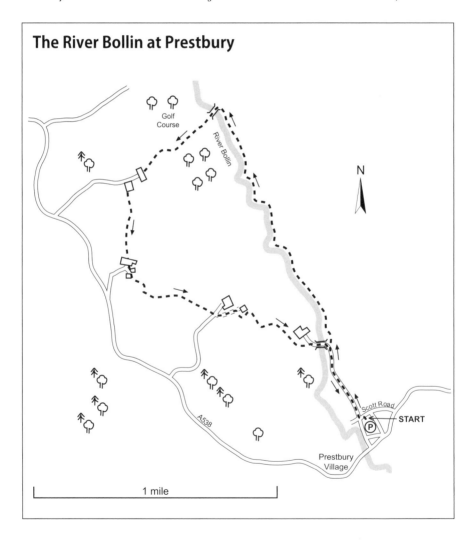

The River Bollin at Prestbury

Bridge over the River Bollin

Go through the farm yard, with the farm buildings on your left. Cross a stile into the field. Continue on with the hedge on your left. Halfway up the field there is a stile on your left. Cross this and then turn right. Continue straight on uphill with the hedge now on your right. Cross another stile and then go straight across the next field.

This brings you onto the driveway of Legh Hall. Continue straight on, with the house and its garden on your right. When you reach a T-junction, with the ménage straight ahead, turn left. Follow the path through the grounds of this house and back out into a field. Head diagonally right, following the footpath sign. This brings you over to the hedge on the right side of the field. Follow the path, with the hedge on your right. Continue to follow the footpath straight on across several fields, until you cross a stile into Greendale Lane.

The lane on the right leads to the main road. On the left the lane forks. The left fork leads to a house. The right fork leads to large electrically

The path leading back to Prestbury Village

operated wooden gates. At the right side of these gates is a stile. Cross over here and walk down the driveway on the other side of the gates. When you reach the complex of buildings, stables, and ménage, the footpath turns right and goes uphill. This path skirts round the perimeter of the property, and turns left at the top of the slope, then heads downhill. At the bottom of the slope, walk straight ahead along a path which is fenced on both sides. You will pass a small pond on your left where you can always see waterfowl, and straight ahead is an excellent view. The fenced path then turns right.

Continue downhill, following the path. It will take you over a footbridge crossing a stream. On the other side, go up some large earth steps, edged with wood. At the top, the path turns right to follow the stream, then after a few yards crosses a stile into a field. On the other side of this stile turn left. Cross two fields following the hedge on your left, and then you will come to a driveway. On the left it leads to Spittle House. Turn right onto the driveway. Go over the bridge across the River Bollin, and then continue back along the route you took at the beginning.

Refreshments

You can get a very good pub lunch at the Admiral Rodney. It is a charming old world pub, with low beams and lots of character. It is on the main road, just after where you entered the car park. The easiest entrance is from the back, where a lane keeps you away from the traffic on the main road.

Ye Olde Admiral Rodney Inn, New Road, Prestbury, Macclesfield SK10 4HP

19. Lindow Common to Morley Green

This walk goes through Lindow Common, and past Black Lake. The walk is quite flat and easy, with no stiles, and mostly on wide paths. There is one small hill, which gives such a surprisingly good view, that it is difficult to believe that you are so near to the centre of Wilmslow.

Lindow common is the site where archaeologists found 'Lindow Man' in a peat bog. He had been perfectly preserved for about 2,000 years. He was taken to a museum in London, but has on occasion been sent to Manchester for a while, to enable local people to see him.

Distance	3¼ miles
Allow	1 hour 40 minutes
Terrain	The footpaths on this walk stay dry even after rain. There are no stiles on this walk.
By car	From Macclesfield, take the A537, travelling west towards Knutsford. At Monks Heath crossroads turn right onto the A34. This takes you into Wilmslow. In the centre of Wilmslow turn left onto the A538 which goes towards Manchester Airport. As you leave Wilmslow the road will run along the side of Lindow Common which is on your left. At the end of the common, turn left into Racecourse Road. The Boddington Arms pub will be on your right, and on your left, a small car park. Park here.
Map	Philip's Ordnance Survey Street Atlas Cheshire Page 59 F4

The walk

With your back to the road, walk through a gap in the fence which takes you onto a path. There is a notice board on your right which gives some information on the area. Go straight on. When you come to a fork in the path take the left fork. When you next come to a place where the main path turns right, but a minor path goes straight on, turn right. This path brings you out at Black Lake. (Note that the path that you should stay on from the car park to the lake, has a yellow surface. The other paths are not surfaced.)

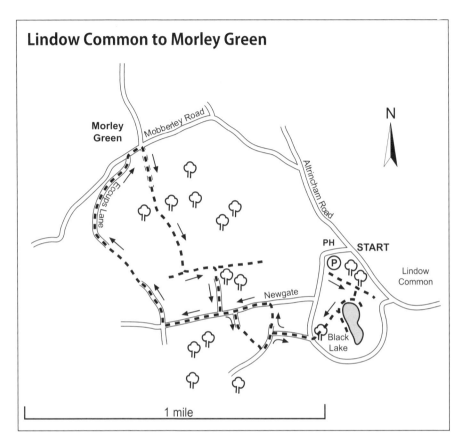

Lindow Common to Morley Green

Morley Green

Mobberley Road

Eccups Lane

Altrincham Road

N

PH

START

Lindow Common

Newgate

Black Lake

1 mile

When you reach the lake, turn right. (If you would like a longer walk you could turn left and walk around the lake.) Walking with the lake on your left, pass four seats. The name on the fourth is Emerson. There is a small group of silver birch trees alongside the seat. Turn right here onto a small narrow footpath which passes between bushes. On the other side of the bushes you come out onto open heath land and immediately cross a path at a crossroads of footpaths. A little further on you will cross another path. You will come out of Lindow Common at a stile, onto Racecourse Road, which is a circular road surrounding the common.

Go straight across the road and up Lindow Lane, which ends in a T-junction with a bridle path on your right. Go through the gate on your right into the bridle path and then follow it until it comes out onto a narrow

Black Lake

road called Newgate. Turn left onto this road. Walk along this road until you reach a crossroads where the main road is on your right. Turn right here. After a short while this is no longer surfaced, and just becomes a dirt track. It goes downhill then up again. You will then be following water in a drainage ditch on your right and some houses on your left. It is quite attractive, and you can spot the marsh marigolds that grow wild here.

This path becomes a tarmaced lane again where there is a small estate of attractive prefabricated houses on your left. These houses are brought on a lorry, lowered into place, then the garden built up around them. The road you are now walking on is called Eccups Lane. You will pass some larger houses then come out on Mobberley Road. You are now in Morley Green.

Turn right onto Mobberley Road, then very shortly afterwards turn right into a lane. Go straight on, downhill, through some trees, and then the path goes uphill. From this point the path has a surface of stones. You will come to a wide grassy open area on your left, while the stony path continues straight on. Turn left onto the wide grassy area and continue up to the top of the hill. At the top you come to an unexpectedly good view. This area is reclaimed land. It used to be Wilmslow tip, but was turned into a wildlife and recreational area. You will see some metal covers, where the ground can be monitored as it settles.

When you walk down the other side of the hill you will see a fenced area ahead of you. Head towards this. Do not take the path on the left which just leads back to the main road. When you reach the fenced area you will see that to the left of the fence is a path which runs down the side of the fenced area. You can either follow this footpath or go along the bridle path through the fenced area. This brings you back to Newgate, where you turn left.

Within a few yards you turn right into a lane which immediately becomes a tree-lined bridleway. It is very pleasant walking here. Look out for the

Lindow Common

bluebells on the grassy banks in the spring. You will come to a place where a lane crosses this bridleway. On your right you will see some stables, and beyond that a white detached house. Turn left here. Pass a large garden and a house on your left. You will come back to Lindow Lane. Turn right onto Lindow Lane, and then retrace your steps back to your car.

Refreshments

Turn right out of the car park then right onto the A538, which takes you back to Wilmslow. At the traffic lights in the centre of Wilmslow turn right. Immediately after you pass Sainsbury's on your left, turn left into the car park of the Coach and Four. This is a very old pub with lots of character, where you can enjoy an excellent lunch in congenial surroundings.

The Coach and Four, 69-71 Alderley Road, Wilmslow SK9 1PA

20. Brereton Heath to Swettenham

This walk is ideal for the spring when you can enjoy the daffodils and spring flowers.

There is a quaint old ford. They are rare now, but they used to be commonplace on country roads.

The walk goes through some beautiful Cheshire countryside. It imparts a feeling of peace and serenity. The roads and paths have remained unchanged for a great many years. Some of the trees are very old and have seen much of our history.

Distance	4½ miles
Allow	2 hour 20 minutes
Terrain	This walk stays dry underfoot. The display of daffodils are worth seeing early in April, followed by primroses in mid-April.
By car	From Macclesfield, take Congleton Road, the A536, travelling south. At Congleton turn left onto the A34 through Congleton. When you reach the large roundabout at the other side of Congleton, take the 3rd exit off the roundabout, which is the A54 to Holmes Chapel. Follow this road for 4 ½ miles to Brereton Heath. On the right you will see a large brown sign saying 'Brereton Heath Country Park'. Turn left here. This is Davenport Lane. 200 yards down this road on the left you will find an entrance into the car park of the country park. It is a Pay and Display car park.
Map	Philip's Ordnance Survey Street Atlas Cheshire Page 154 B4

The walk

First take time to enjoy the beauty of the lake, then turn, with the lake on your right, and follow the path. Pass the toilet block on your right, and then take the left fork in the path. This leads to a small gate. Go through this to come back into Davenport Lane. Turn right onto this road. Go to the crossroads where you go straight across the main road and into the bridleway opposite.

Brereton Heath to Swettenham

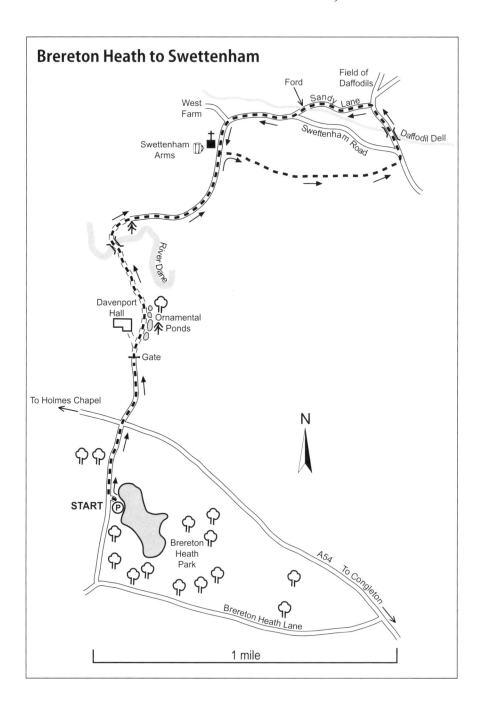

Field of Daffodils

Ford

Sandy Lane

West Farm

Swettenham Road

Daffodil Dell

Swettenham Arms

River Dane

Davenport Hall

Ornamental Ponds

Gate

To Holmes Chapel

N

START P

Brereton Heath Park

A54 To Congleton

Brereton Heath Lane

1 mile

The bridleway starts as a tarmac lane, and then after about 200 yards you pass through a large white gate, after which the surface changes to stones in the centre with verges of grass. In the spring there are daffodils on the bank on the other side of the fence on your left. You will pass two gates with driveways on your left. They both lead to Davenport Hall. The bridleway then heads downhill past a series of four ornamental ponds on your right.

At the bottom of the slope, the path crosses over a bridge across the River Dane. This is a very picturesque spot. On a sunny day in the spring the sun will glint off all the little white tops of the water as it rushes over stones on the riverbed. The large mature willow tree which overhangs the river will be a beautiful golden colour as it is just coming into leaf again after its winter sleep. After crossing the river you head uphill once more. You will pass a large house on the left then go through another large white gate. Continue onwards on the tarmac lane into Swettenham.

The River Dane at Brereton

The first thing you see in Swettenham is the cemetery on your right. But it is so hidden behind hedges that you will only see the name on the gate. You will pass some primroses on the grass verge, then next, there is a church on your left, and behind that is the Swettenham Arms. On the right hand side of the road is a stile. Cross this, then walk along a path between two fences which opens out onto a field. Continue straight on, heading towards two very large old trees, which are one behind the other so that at first you can only see one tree. Pass them on your left and then continue to walk straight on, with a fence on your left. After crossing a second field, you will pass another large, ancient tree on your left.

Keep straight on, following the fence on your left until you reach the fourth field, where the fence curves away to the left. Do not follow it, but go straight across the field. You come to a stile next to a wrought iron gate. Cross this stile.

On your right is Congleton Road. On your left there are two roads. The nearest is Swettenham Lane and the one further on is the other half of Congleton Road. Turn left into Congleton Road and then head downhill. At the bottom of the slope, the road crosses Swettenham brook. This little stream leads into the river Dane. All the verges here are covered in daffodils in the spring, and it is worth stopping on the bridge to enjoy the picturesque valley that the brook tumbles through. Continue onwards, uphill a short distance to Sandy Lane on your left. Turn left. On your right you will see a spectacular field full of daffodils.

Follow this lane downhill. Don't miss the primroses on the bank on your right. At the bottom of the slope you will be joined by Swettenham brook on your left. It follows you for a few yards then turns right to go under the bridge which carries your path. As you cross the bridge, look to your right to see the white wood anemones under the trees. The road traffic has to go through the ford. Just the other side is a sign which says 'Now try your brakes.' That is a road sign you don't see very often. Continue straight on, heading uphill once more. On the verge on your right you will see lots of Celandine - small pretty yellow flowers. At the top of the slope you turn right into Swettenham Lane, which comes in on your left.

Continue straight on along Swettenham Lane. A short way along this road it takes a left turn. On your right the side road is a dead end and just leads to a farm, so stay on the main road. This brings you back to the

The ford at Swettenham

church and the Swettenham Arms which you passed earlier. You then retrace your outwards route.

Refreshments

Head back towards Congleton. Go around the large roundabout back onto the A34. At the next roundabout turn left into Obelisk Way and then turn left into the Cheshire Tavern which has a fine selection of meals, and often has an offer of two for the price of one.

Cheshire Tavern, West Road, Congleton CW12 4EY

21. Rudyard Lake

This walk goes round Rudyard Lake, which can be viewed from many points on your route. The lake is very picturesque, especially so from the south end, where there are many small boats and there are also wildfowl to watch or to feed, and there is also a visitors centre and a café.

The higher ground on the west side of the lake gives beautiful views of a very typical English pastoral scene.

The Rudyard Lake Steam Railway starts from the little train station then runs along the side of Rudyard Lake. The trains run mostly at weekends, on bank holidays and in school holidays. If you would like, you could combine a walk round most of the lake, with a return on the miniature train.

This walk has the advantage of having only one stile.

Distance	4 miles
Allow	2 hours
Terrain	The footpaths on this walk stay dry after wet weather. From the middle of May, the rhododendrons are in flower by the dam. There is a lot of shade on this walk on bright sunny summer days.
By car	From Macclesfield, take the A523 towards Leek. Go straight across Bosley crossroads, through Rushton Spencer, and then take a right turn into Rudyard, onto Rudyard Road, the B5331. When you go under the railway bridge, turn left immediately, and then go up the one-way drive into the car park of the miniature railway.
Map	Philip's Ordnance Survey Street Atlas Staffs Page 29 F8

The walk

From the train station follow the tracks over the road and then onwards until you reach the dam on your left. Turn left here and then go across the

Rudyard Lake

dam. When you reach the other side, go straight on. There are two tracks ahead. The one on the left curves off to the left. Take the one on the right which goes straight up a small slope to the road. At the road turn right.

Or, after walking past the dam, turn right, pass the visitors centre on your right, the toilets and the café on your left, then turn left and go up a path to the road. At the road turn right.

Follow the road for a short distance to where it forks. The right fork is a cul-de-sac called The Crescent, which just leads to some houses. Take the left fork, which is a stony track going up a slope. After a short distance this divides. The track which curves off to the right is used by cars. Take the footpath on the left. Continue along here until it reaches a lane. Turn right onto the lane, which leads to houses. Continue on along the path past the houses. After a little while this brings you out onto another lane. Turn right onto the lane.

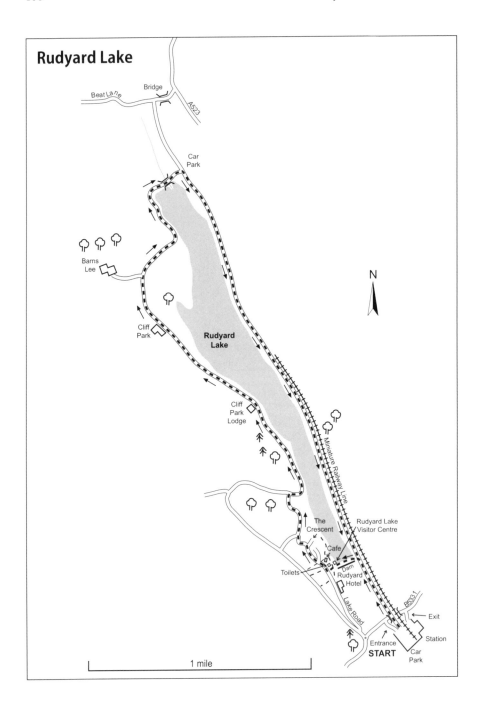

Rudyard Lake

Beat Lane
Bridge
A523
Car Park
Barns Lee
Cliff Park
Rudyard Lake
Cliff Park Lodge
Miniature Railway Line
The Crescent
Rudyard Lake Visitor Centre
Cafe
Toilets
Dam
Rudyard Hotel
Lake Road
B5331
Exit
Station
Entrance
Car Park
START

N

1 mile

Cliffe Park

After a while you will pass the Cliffe Park Lodge. This is a castellated building which has a wide front but very shallow depth. After walking on a little further, you will reach a large castellated building, which is called Cliffe Park. The path you are on goes across its front lawn. There is a gate leading onto it and another as you leave it.

Continue on along the path. From the lake up until now your path has been mostly through woods, but it now opens out into beautiful panoramic views. A little distance further on you turn right onto a path which is the driveway up to a farm called Barns Lee, on your left. This path takes you to a bridge over the stream which feeds the reservoir, then on to the car park at the north end of the lake. The car park consists of two lay-bys off a small lane. You could park here and start the walk from here.

Turn right here, and then pass under an old stone bridge. You are now on the path of what used to be a railway. The path goes straight down the east side of the lake. Halfway along this side you will come to the last station of the little Rudyard Lake Steam Railway. Follow the railway tracks back to the car park.

Refreshments

You can get a very nice lunch at the Rudyard Hotel. From the car park of the miniature train station, go down the one-way exit drive to the road and turn left. At the mini-roundabout turn right. Just after the mini-roundabout there is a fork, take the road on the right. After a short distance the Rudyard Hotel is on your right.

Alternatively, you could drive back to Rushton Spencer then turn into the first road on the left, which is Station Lane. A little way up there, on the left is the Knot Inn where you can have lunch.

Alternate parking

If you intend having lunch at The Rudyard Hotel, you could park there, by arrangement with the staff, and start the walk from there. Or, you could park at the visitors centre and start the walk from there. Alternatively you could start the walk from the north end of the lake.

To the car park at the north end of the lake

When you reach the far end of Rushton Spencer, the road which goes straight on is signposted to Heaton. The main road which you are on, the A523, turns right. Keep on this main road. It curves a bit and then you come to a road on your right. Turn right into this road, which is called Beat Lane. After a very short distance the road goes over a small bridge. Just the other side of this bridge is a narrow lane on the left. Turn left into this lane. You will need to drive slowly down it and beware of potholes and sleeping policemen. At the other end it forks, but just before the fork there are two lay-bys on your left where you can park.

Rudyard Hotel, Lake Road, Rudyard, Leek, Staffordshire AT13 8RN
Knot Inn, Station Lane, Rushton Spencer, Nr Macclesfield SK11 0QU

22. Twinnies Bridge

The first part of this walk goes along a very attractive path which leads from Twinnies Bridge to Quarry Bank Mill in Styal Country Park. It then proceeds onwards to Morley. The last half of the walk is along a very picturesque path through Styal woods, mostly following the River Bollin. Much of this walk follows the 'Bollin Valley Way'.

Styal Country Park and Quarry Bank Mill belong to the National Trust.

Distance	3½ miles
Allow	1¾ hours
Terrain	This walk is suitable all year round.
By car	Take the Silk Road (A523) northwards out of Macclesfield. Take the left turning into Prestbury. Go straight through the village. At the far end take the right turning and go up Castle Hill. Continue on this road until you reach the Wilmslow by-pass, the A34. Turn right onto this road. At the next roundabout turn left and go under the railway bridge to a roundabout where you turn right. Then turn left into the next main road on your left, which is Styal Road (B5166). Continuing along Styal Road you will pass on your left, Cliff Road and Bollin Hill together, then the other part of Bollin Hill, then Grange Park Avenue cul-de-sac, then you come to the car park at Twinnies Bridge on your left. Park here.
Map	Philip's Ordnance Survey Street Atlas Cheshire Page 33 F1

The walk

With Styal Road on your right and the bridge on your left, walk straight ahead, passing the brick building on your right. Follow this path all the way to Quarry Bank Mill. Continue on to a fork in the path. The right path goes uphill. Take the left path and walk along the front of the old mill building. At the far end, the path turns left onto a cobbled path. There is a signpost here saying 'To Morley'.

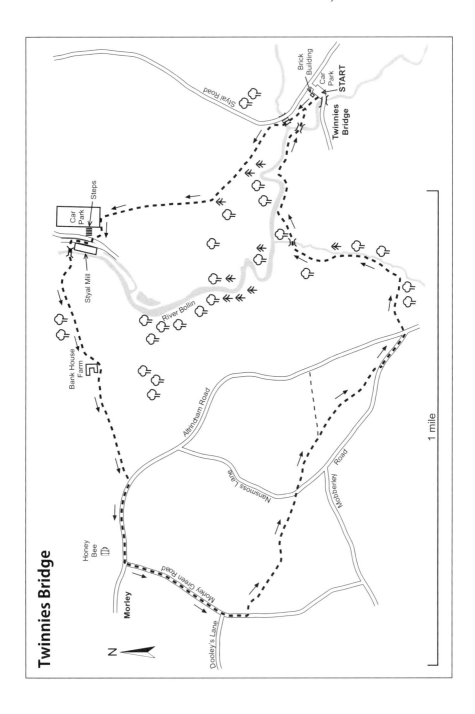

Twinnies Bridge

N

Brick Building

Car Park START

Twinnies Bridge

Styal Road

Steps

Car Park

Styal Mill

River Bollin

Bank House Farm

Altrincham Road

Nansmoss Lane

Mobberley Road

1 mile

Honey Bee

Morley

Morley Green Road

Dooley's Lane

The path crosses the river, where you can see Styal gardens over the water to your right. The path is fenced on both sides. Continue on and then the path turns right and goes uphill for a little distance. It levels out then goes through a farmyard. Across the other side of the farmyard you walk down the drive that leads to the farm, until you reach Altrincham Road.

Styal woods

Turn right onto the road. Pass the Honey Bee pub. Turn left into the next road, which is Morley Green Road. Walk past Dooley's Lane on your right. When you come to some houses on your left, you will find a signpost marking a footpath which runs up the side of the end house. It is quite hidden and overgrown. Turn up this footpath. After a short distance it opens out into a small field. Following the fence on your left, cross another two fields. In the next field you come to a fence which blocks your path. Walk around three sides of the field until you come to a stile with the farmhouse close to the right hand side of it. Cross the stile into the road, which is called Nansmoss Lane.

Go straight across Nansmoss Lane into a wide grassy hedge-lined path. Follow this for a distance. Go straight on at the crossroads of paths. This comes out in Mobberley Road, where you turn left. After a short distance you reach Altrincham Road. Go straight across Altrincham road onto a wide path, which is marked at the start with a signpost saying 'To Twinnies Bridge'. This takes you into Styal Woods.

A short way down this path there is another which comes off on the left. Turn left onto this path. This path follows a ravine. There is quite a drop on your right with a small stream flowing along at the bottom of the slope. The next section of the path crosses several wooden bridges and walkways. There are signs on these telling you that you are on the 'Bollin Valley Way'. When the stream reaches the River Bollin, your path turns right and then follows the river, which is on your left. Continue to follow this path which will cross the river on a footbridge just before you get back to the car park at Twinnies Bridge.

Refreshments
The Coach and Four in Wilmslow is a carvery with an excellent menu. To get there, turn right out of the car park, back onto Styal Road and go to the T-junction with Manchester Road. Turn right and then drive through the centre of Wilmslow until you find the Coach and Four on your left, at the end of the shops.

The Coach and Four, 69-71 Alderley Road, Wilmslow SK9 1PA

23. Astbury Mere Country Park

Asbury Mere County Park is a place of natural beauty. At its centre is the lake which gives it its name. This walk takes you round the lake so that you can enjoy the views across the lake from various different points. There is an abundance of wildfowl which you can observe in different seasons. Also, in the spring it is well worth visiting just to see the wildflower meadow. In front of the church at Astbury there is a spectacular display of daffodils in April.

Distance	3¾ miles
Allow	1 hour 50 minutes
Terrain	This walk is best in early April when the daffodils are spectacular, or early in June to see the wild orchids in the wildflower meadow. There are no stiles on this walk.
By car	From Macclesfield take the road to Congleton. This will join the A34 just before you reach Congleton. Stay on the A34 until you are leaving Congleton. Just after the 2nd roundabout turn left into Sandy Lane. There is a brown sign pointing down this road which says 'Asbury Mere Country Park'. Go to the end of Sandy Lane and into the car park.
Map	Philip's Ordnance Survey Street Atlas Cheshire Page 156 A1

The walk

Walk along the path with the mere on your right. There are two paths going in this direction. If you take the higher one, you will get a better view of the mere and surrounding countryside and the hills beyond. You will also pass alongside the wild flower meadow. When your path divides, take the right turning and keep walking round the lake. On the opposite side of the lake the path will leave the lake and take you to the main road (A34).

Go straight across the road and straight on, down the road opposite which is Padgbury Lane. When this divides, take the road on the left, which is also called Padgbury Lane. After a few yards turn right, where there is a footpath

The spring display of daffodils at Astbury

sign on a signpost. Walk up this path, which is only a few yards long and you reach two small gates. Take the one on the right. Following the direction shown by the sign at the gate, head slightly to the right across a small field. Then go across a little bridge over a stream. On the other side of the bridge turn left. Follow this path until it brings you out onto Bent Lane. Turn left and then go down this lane, back to the main road (A34).

Go straight across and slightly to the right, then up the road which is nearly opposite Bent lane. There will be a grassy triangle on your right. After passing the triangle, and the large church on your right, the road forks. Take the road on the left, which is School Lane. Staying on School Lane, go past the driveway on the left which leads to houses and a footpath. Then you will come to two farm gates. The one on the left leads to Brickhouse Farm. Go through the one on the right. Walk in the direction shown by the footpath arrow on the gate. This takes you diagonally left to a small gate into the second field.

The second field is quite large. Follow the hedge on your left. Halfway across the field the hedge is recessed. There is a small gate on your left here, which leads onto another footpath. Go past this and continue in the same direction as you have been walking.

A small gate leads you into the third field. Walking straight on follow a stream on your left, which is at the bottom of a slope. When you reach the other side of this small field, you will see on your left a small bridge over the stream. Turn left; go down the slope and over the bridge. The path then takes you up 22 steps and opens out onto one of the fairways on a golf course.

Walk straight across the fairway. On the other side of the fairway is a path to your right and left and straight ahead is a small clump of trees. Turn

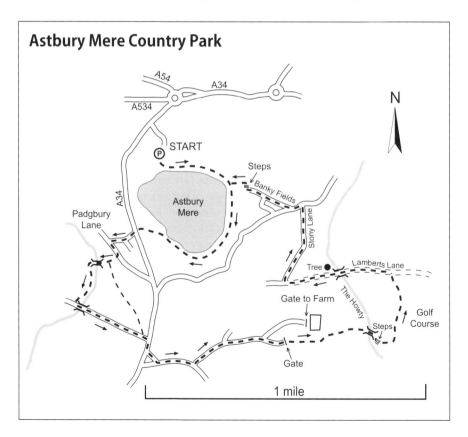

Astbury Mere

left onto this path and then continue straight on. This takes you through a small clump of trees then across a second fairway. On the far side of this second fairway you walk over a small concrete bridge over a stream and then into a small wood. The path brings you out on a third fairway. Continue straight on, following a line of four oak trees, which are marked with yellow footpath markers. This brings you to a fourth fairway. Continue straight on across the fourth fairway. This brings you to a path through a wood. As you enter the wood you are leaving the golf course.

Continue along this well defined path, which is wide and tree lined and leads you to a T-junction of paths. Turn left. Continue along this path, past the footpath on the right which is marked with a signpost. You come to a bridge over a stream where a footpath continues on over the bridge, but there is also a footpath which turns right, just before the stream. Take this right turning. You will immediately have to go round a very large tree which has grown over the path before curving upwards.

After the tree, continue along this path until you go through a small gate to a junction where there is a path on your left, and another straight on, but you take the one which curves round so sharply to your right that you are almost walking back in the direction you came. But after a few yards it curves to your left and goes uphill.

A little further on turn left onto Waggs Road then right into Bankyfields. When Bankyfields curves to the left, continue straight on along a wide path, which then continues as a narrow path. After a few yards turn right and go down 26 steps. There is a path which goes across the bottom of these steps. Turn left onto this path. The path then goes down another 15 steps. When you reach the mere take the path to the right, which takes you back to the car park.

Refreshments
You can have a very good lunch at the Egerton Arms at Astbury. You go back to the A34 and turn left then go to Astbury, where the Egerton Arms is on your left.

Or you can lunch at the Cheshire Tavern. For the Cheshire Tavern drive back to the A34 and turn right. At the second roundabout turn left into Obelisk Way, then turn left into the Cheshire Tavern.

Egerton Arms Country Inn, Astbury Village, Congleton CW12 4RQ
Cheshire Tavern, West Road, Congleton CW12 4EY

24. Dun Cow, Ollerton

This walk starts at the Dun Cow pub, which is between Chelford and Knutsford. The route will take you through some picturesque woods, and through the beautiful Cheshire countryside, on a gentle walk. There are few stiles on this walk. Mostly it follows easy pathways. It is sheltered for most of its length, so is ideal if the day is windy, or a little too sunny.

Distance	**4¼ miles**
Allow	**2 hours 10 minutes**
Terrain	**Ideal choice of walk on a windy day, because most of it is sheltered. Also it provides shade on hot sunny days.**
By car	**From Macclesfield take Chelford Road (A537). Go straight across the Monks Heath crossroads, then straight on at Chelford roundabout, then on Knutsford Road through Chelford. Just before Knutsford you come into Ollerton. Just after you pass the crossroads which has Seven Sisters Lane on the left, you will see the Dun Cow pub on your right. Turn right, into its car park.**
Map	**Philip's Ordnance Survey Street Atlas Cheshire Page 82 C3**

The walk

On leaving the Dun Cow, turn right, onto Chelford Road. Continue along here until the road bends sharply to the right. Just after the bend you will see a stile on the other side of the road. Cross the road and then go over the stile into Windmill Wood. The main path goes straight on, but there is a much narrower path which comes off on the right. Take this narrow path. In the centre of the path you will pass a small standing stone with the name 'Booth' inscribed on it. At first the narrow path goes in the same direction as the main path, but after a while they diverge. Continue straight on until the path brings you out into Gough's Lane.

The path behind The Dun Cow

Turn right into Gough's Lane. Follow this road to the roundabout at Chelford Road. Go straight across at the roundabout. Pass the turning on the left which leads to Booths Hall. Continue straight on through the commercial estate, then past Booth Hall Farm on your right.

Continue straight on across the field. At the other side turn left through a small gate and then right, and then continue straight on until you cross a stream and then go through a gate into a lane. When you walk up this lane you pass some buildings on your right. The lane ends at these buildings, so by continuing straight on you will be crossing a field. After a second field you reach a hedge at the other side, where there is no forward path. Turn right here. Walk halfway along this side of the field, and then turn right at two signposts marked with footpath arrows. Go straight across the field, and then over a stile into woods. Go straight on through the woods.

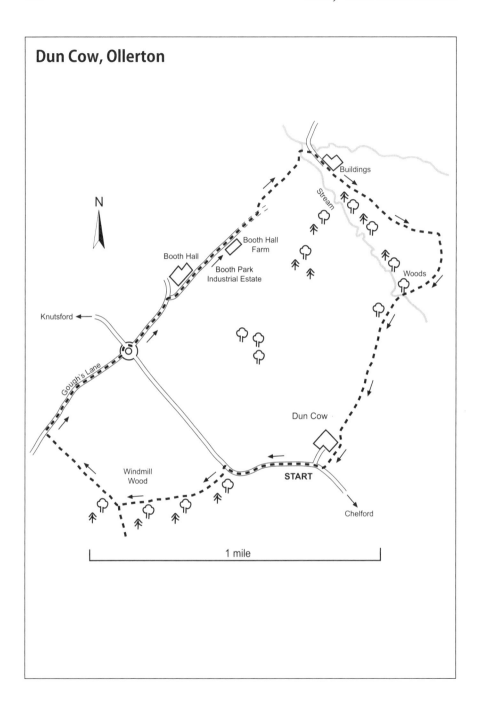

Dun Cow, Ollerton

N

Buildings

Stream

Woods

Booth Hall
Farm

Booth Hall

Booth Park
Industrial Estate

Knutsford

Gough's Lane

Dun Cow

Windmill
Wood

START

Chelford

1 mile

After a while the path comes out of the woods. Continue to follow the path straight on. The path eventually comes to the Dun Cow pub. You will see its car park straight ahead, but there is no entrance to it here. You will need to turn left, and then circle round the pub, following the path, until you come back to Chelford Road, then turn right to come into the pub.

Refreshments
You can get a good lunch at the Dun Cow. You will need to check whether it is alright to park here while you are on your walk.

Dun Cow, Chelford Road, Ollerton, Knutsford WA16 8RH

The Dun Cow

25. North Rode

This walk takes you past the flight of 12 locks at Bosley on the Macclesfield canal, which is part of the Cheshire ring, where you can watch the picturesque narrow boats navigating the locks and cruising serenely along the canal.

You will also get an excellent view of the viaduct, firstly from a distance and then as you get closer you will become aware of its enormous size. The viaduct is a fantastic feat of Victorian engineering with its 20 arches. It carries the main Macclesfield railway line over the valley of the River Dane.

Distance	4 miles
Allow	2 hours
Terrain	This walk is most enjoyable in the summer when there are lots of colourful narrow boats using the locks on the canal.
By car	From Macclesfield take London Road (A523) south. Shortly after you pass the Lyme Green Business Park on your right, you will find that Macclesfield canal is following your road on your right. Once you pass the Fools Nook pub on your left, and a swing bridge over the canal on your right, you take the second road on your right, which is Bull Gate Lane. There is a sign here for North Rode. A short distance down Bull Gate Lane there is a lay-by on the right, next to the canal, where you can park.
Map	Philip's Ordnance Survey Street Atlas Cheshire Page 135 D2

The walk

Go down onto the canal towpath from where your road crosses the canal. Head south. The water in the canal will be on your left. The bridge where you came onto the canal is number 54. Walk past the locks. After you have passed number 5, you will go under bridge number 55, which carries the A54 road to Congleton. Continue on past the remaining 6 locks. After you have passed the last one, number 12, the Macclesfield canal will then cross over the River Dane. You will be able to see it far below you. Immediately after that you come to bridge number 57, which carries a grassy footpath over the canal. Turn right onto this footpath.

The footpath becomes a well-defined track. Continue straight on. After about 10 minutes you will see the viaduct ahead of you. Continue on until you pass under the viaduct. On the other side, go through a farm gate which brings you into the yard of Woodward's Heavy Haulage. Continue straight on down the road to the main road, the A54 Congleton Road. Turn right onto the A54. In less than five minutes you will reach a narrow bridge which takes the A54 over the River Dane. There are traffic lights which only allow traffic in one direction at a time. Cross this bridge. Half way across, there are wider places on both sides where pedestrians can stand while traffic passes. On the other side of the bridge turn immediately left and cross over a stile.

Canal bridges framing walkers

After a short distance your path will take you over a narrow footbridge which crosses a stream. Then when the path divides, turn right. After the path crosses two fields it brings you out onto Church Lane. Turn left. The road bends to the right, then to the left. You then turn right into a lane, which has the church on your right, and a small, old school on your left. This is the centre of North Rode village.

After passing the church on your right, you will pass a B&B on your right, then go through a farm gate and continue on along a path. When the path forks, keep to the right. After crossing fields the path takes you to a stile which you cross onto a surfaced track. On the left there is a farm gate

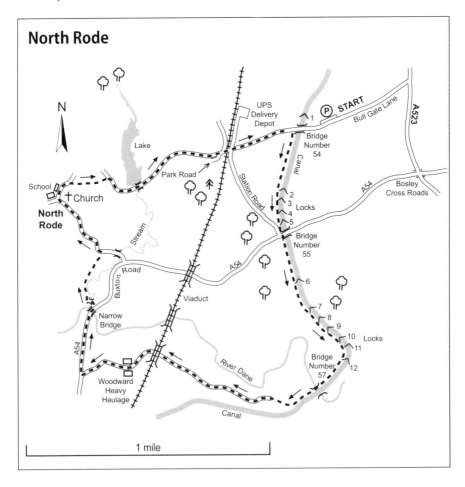

Narrow boat and walkers on the Macclesfield canal

across the track. Turn right here and follow this track. At the start of it you pass a lake on your left.

After about ten minutes you come out onto a bend on the main road. Continue straight on. The road crosses the railway line. Just the other side of the railway is Station Road on your right, and the driveway into a delivery firm on your left. Continue straight on past both of these. You are now on the road where you parked, and after a short walk you will come back to your car.

Refreshments

You can have a very good lunch at the Knot Inn at Rushton Spencer. Drive back to the Macclesfield to Leek Road, the A523, and turn right. Go straight across at the traffic lights at Bosley Crossroads. When you reach Rushton Spencer turn right into Station Lane. The Knot Inn is on your left.

Knot Inn, Station Lane, Rushton Spencer, Nr Macclesfield SK11 0QU

Addresses of pubs recommended in this book:

Blacksmiths Arms, Chelford Road, Henbury, Macclesfield SK11 9PG

Cheshire Tavern, West Road, Congleton CW12 4EY

Church House, Sutton Lane, Sutton Lane Ends, Macclesfield SK11 0DS

Church House Inn, 24 Church Street, Bollington SK10 5PY

Coach and Four The, 69-71 Alderley Road, Wilmslow SK9 1PA

Cock and Pheasant, 15 Bollington Road, Bollington, Macclesfield SK10 5EJ

Cock The, Chelford Road, Henbury, Macclesfield, Cheshire SK10 3LH

Davenport Arms, Congleton Road, Marton, Macclesfield SK11 9HF

Dog Inn The, Wellbank Lane, Over Peover, Knutsford WA16 8UP

Dun Cow, Chelford Road, Ollerton, Knutsford WA16 8RH

Egerton Arms Country Inn, Astbury Village, Congleton CW12 4RQ

Flower Pot, 1 Congleton Road, Macclesfield SK11 7UF

Knot Inn, Station Lane, Rushton Spencer, Nr Macclesfield SK11 0QU

Legh Arms, London Road, Adlington, Macclesfield SK10 4NA

Miners Arms, Wood Lane North, Adlington, Macclesfield SK10 4PF

Red Lion Inn, Station Road, Goostrey, CW4 8PJ

Rising Sun, Congleton Road, Macclesfield SK11 7XD

Robin Hood Inn, Buxton Road, Buglawton, Congleton CW12 3PE

Robin Hood Inn The, Church Lane, Rainow, Macclesfield SK10 5XE

Rudyard Hotel, Lake Road, Rudyard, Leek, Staffordshire AT13 8RN

Vernon Arms, London Road South, Poynton, Stockport SK12 1LQ

Wagon and Horses, Manchester Road (A34), Eaton, Nr.Congleton, CW12 2JD

Wizard The, Macclesfield Road, Nether Alderley SK10 4UB

Ye Olde Admiral Rodney Inn, New Road, Prestbury, Macclesfield SK10 4HP

Ye Olde Parkgate Inn, Stocks Lane, Over Peover, Knutsford WA16 8TU

Also from Sigma Leisure:

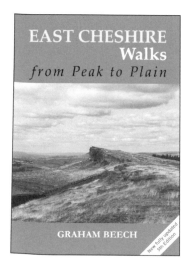

East Cheshire Walks from Peak to Plain
Graham Beech

East Cheshire is a land of contracts — from rugged hills to gently rolling countryside. Thanks to this variety, there really is something for walkers of all interests and abilities — and *East Cheshire Walks* is by far the most comprehensive guidebook to the area, with almost 40 walks ranging from 3 to 20 miles covering a total of over 250 miles. There are easy ambles in Cheshire's mid-county pasture land, interesting strolls alongside rivers and canals, and a selection of more strenuous hikes in the foothills of the Peak District.

£8.99

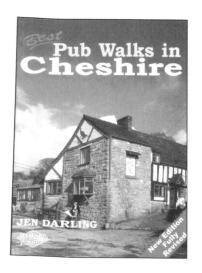

Best Pub Walks in Cheshire 2nd Edition
Jen Darling

This is the second edition of a guidebook to the walks and pubs of Cheshire.

"I was delighted to be asked to put a few words on paper … this book brings together a series of suggestions for your enjoyment."
– John Ellis, Cheshire Tourism

£8.99

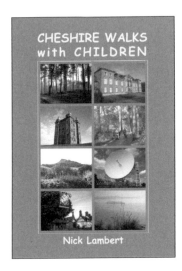

Cheshire Walks With Children 2nd Edition
Nick Lambert

Now completely revised and updated, this was the first in our "walks with children" series and has quickly become a firm favourite. There are 30 walks, ranging in length, together with things to look out for and questions to answer along the way make it an entertaining book for young and old alike.

£8.99

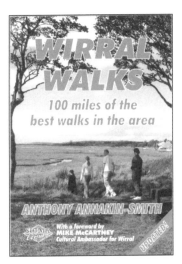

Wirral Walks 2nd Edition
100 miles of the best walks in the area
Anthony Annakin-Smith

A completely revised and updated edition of this popular collection of 25 walks from around 2 to 10 miles, covering a total of 100 miles through the best of the local landscape. The author's careful research highlights the interesting and unusual features seen along each route.

£8.99

All of our books are all available on-line at **www.sigmapress.co.uk** or through booksellers. For a free catalogue, please contact:

Sigma Leisure, Stobart House, Pontyclerc, Penybanc Road, Ammanford, Carmarthenshire SA18 3HP
Tel: 01269 593100   Fax: 01269 596116

info@sigmapress.co.uk   www.sigmapress.co.uk